Europe

THE EUROPE WE NEED

Leon Brittan

HAMISH HAMILTON · LONDON

HAMISH HAMILTON LTD

Published by the Penguin Group
Penguin Books Ltd, 27 Wrights Lane, London w8 5tz, England
Penguin Books USA Inc., 375 Hudson Street, New York, New York 10014, USA
Penguin Books Australia Ltd, Ringwood, Victoria, Australia
Penguin Books Canada Ltd, 10 Alcorn Avenue, Toronto, Ontario, Canada m4v 3b2
Penguin Books (NZ) Ltd, 182–190 Wairau Road, Auckland 10, New Zealand

Penguin Books Ltd, Registered Offices: Harmondsworth, Middlesex, England

First published 1994

5 7 9 10 8 6 4

Typeset by Datix International Limited, Bungay, Suffolk
Printed in England by Clays Ltd, St Ives plc
Filmset in 11½/14 pt Monophoto Bembo

A CIP catalogue record for this book is available from the British Library
ISBN 0-241-00249-4

EUROPE

Contents

CONTENTS

Acknowledgements

Although I, of course, take full and sole responsibility for the contents of this book it has in truth been very much a collaborative effort.

The ideas put forward are ones that I have been mulling over for a long time, in some cases years. They have been formed as a result of my own experience in the European Commission, and after talking about the issues raised in various ways and at various times with a very wide variety of people in public life, in business, in academic life and in the media all over Europe and beyond.

The ideas were then winnowed down and produced in their present form by means of extensive discussions with the present members of my personal staff in Brussels, my 'Cabinet', as it is called, and with their very active assistance in preparing the text. Warm thanks are therefore due to Colin Budd, my Chef de Cabinet, Catherine Day, my Deputy Chef de Cabinet, and the other members of the Cabinet, namely David Coyne, Robert Madelin, Alison Hook, David Wright and Anna Barnett. I am also grateful to the former members of my Cabinet, Jonathan Faull and Martin Donnelly, for their advice and assistance.

A special word of thanks, however, is due to another member of my Brussels team, Peter Guilford, who undertook the daunting task of helping me to hack the ideas that I finally came up with into something capable of being published.

ACKNOWLEDGEMENTS

Finally a word of thanks to Andrew Franklin and Kate Jones of Hamish Hamilton, who enthusiastically encouraged me to write this book in the first place and then helped me to understand what might be of interest and comprehensible to possible readers, and what was too esoteric to be of interest to anyone other than European aficionados.

CHAPTER I

What Kind of Europe Do
We Need?

More than at any time since 1945, Europe has in the last year or so been racked by self-doubt and unsure about its future direction. A new crisis of identity has crept across the continent, as people question the purpose and proper role of the European Union,* as well as their country's role in Europe and Europe's status in the wider world. The root cause is clear: two halves of an old continent have been thrust back together after forty-five years apart, colliding traumatically with the worst economic downturn the world has witnessed since the Great Depression. But we must carry out a fuller diagnosis of Europe's current ills if we are to be serious about finding a lasting cure.

The shock that has hit the continent has, of course, been greater in Eastern Europe, where in addition to the advent of

* Under the Maastricht Treaty, the signatory states formed the European Union, embracing all existing policies of the European Community, but incorporating two new 'pillars' as well: firstly a Common Foreign and Security Policy and secondly Justice and Home Affairs. All three are now part of the Union, a term first used in the Solemn Declaration of Stuttgart in 1983 prior to the Single European Act. The main procedural difference is that in areas of 'Community' activity, the European Commission has the sole right to initiate proposals, whereas in the other two, that right is shared with the member states. The term 'European Union' has caught on quickly as an overall replacement for the 'European Community'. For the sake of clarity and simplicity, I propose to use the term 'Union' except where it is plainly misleading or inaccurate to do so, in which case I revert to 'Community'.

I

war, people's aspirations for democracy and material prosperity are proving far harder to satisfy than had seemed likely when the Iron Curtain fell. But in the West, if the pain itself has not been as intense, the effect is proving to be equally profound. It may not have forced such dramatic changes on people's daily lives, but it has set about undermining many cherished beliefs about the rightful place of their country in Europe.

The collapse of the Soviet empire has altered the entire European landscape, burying simple if dangerous certainties based on nuclear deterrence and forcing us to contemplate a less polarized, more unstable world. The common enemy has gone, only to be replaced by a far less conspicuous enemy within, as ethnic, national and religious tensions spill over into open conflict. The might of the Soviet nuclear arsenal now seems harmless compared to a band of vengeful militiamen in Bosnia, and our seeming incapacity to bring them to justice has rocked our confidence and security.

So great has been the impact of the war in Yugoslavia on public opinion in Western Europe that people are now questioning the institutions which were built as a bulwark against the threat of attack from without. NATO has been engaged in serious analysis about its future role ever since the Cold War began to thaw, and this analysis is intensifying as people ask how it is that such a successful defence system cannot work in a crisis as local as that in the Balkans. The need for the Alliance is as strong as ever, but in what exact shape and capacity people are unsure.

But above all it is the European Union which now finds itself right in the firing line. This is hardly surprising. The Union is the most ambitious and sophisticated experiment in integration ever undertaken between nation states, and it is approaching one of the crucial crossroads in that process. As their trade barriers come down, European nations have begun agonizing over how far to pool their loftier decisions on foreign, economic and security policy, and to what size their Union should ultimately grow.

And yet the very Treaty that was designed to tackle those questions has been criticized from all sides ever since it was agreed in Maastricht in December 1991. For some the Maastricht Treaty threatened to take Europe too far down the road to federalism, while for others it did not go far enough. There are those who say it was conceived before the full implications of the collapse of the Berlin Wall became apparent, and is therefore suitable to the shaping of half a continent, but not of a whole one. Others dismiss it as a messy, incomprehensible patchwork of opt-ins, opt-outs and eleventh-hour compromises. If popular demonology were to be believed, Maastricht will rob Germans of their Deutschmark, Britons of their Parliament and Frenchmen of their farm subsidies, as well as forcing young Danes into a European army under German command.

The Maastricht Treaty itself is not to blame. It just became a magnet for deeper questions about how far European nations should decide things together or separately in response to the reunification of Europe. Maastricht attracted those questions because it confronts the essential fact that the European Union is a political as well as an economic entity.

The Union's purpose has been to cement the peoples of Europe together in a way that would make war unthinkable and impossible. That is a fundamentally political role, even if the tools used by the Union are primarily economic in nature. It is hard for the younger generation to understand the overwhelming desire after the Second World War to end the strife that had devastated Europe for centuries, and to bury the enmity between France and Germany that led to three wars between them, two of them spreading worldwide, in the space of just a century. Today's generation takes the war for granted as a fact of history, but for those who lived through and just after it, the burning need was to build the institutions which would render a repeat impossible. If NATO was the outer wall, then the European Union provided the internal cement, integrating Western Europe's economies to the point where political disagreements would no longer spill over into open conflict.

In fact, those organizations have been so successful in that original mission that some now ask whether they are still needed. NATO, it is said, has seen off the Soviet threat, while the European Union has made such friends of sworn enemies that they can live side by side without needing fresh attempts at further integration. This is a commonly held view, but it is a profoundly misguided one.

For most people at the time, the post-war integration of Europe was not conceived as a one-off exercise but as a longer-term process that would remain sufficiently dynamic and adaptable to prevent unravelling, as well as reflect the changing economic circumstances both inside Western Europe and outside it. Now that the Cold War is over, that adaptability faces its greatest test since the Community was conceived.

As Europe struggles to adapt to this challenge, people are seeing the fabric of their society changing and they cannot work out exactly why. This only deepens their sense of insecurity. Crime, especially in the cities, has greatly increased this feeling of uncertainty. In a broader sense, ideological differences have faded, only to be replaced by ethnic or religious tensions. This in turn has fuelled a new antagonism towards immigrants. While Britain has been learning to deal with the challenges presented by large-scale immigration for many years, some of its continental neighbours have had to face up to the question more recently. In Germany, public anxiety has soared as recession and the collapse of Communism have revived long-held fears of mass migration from the East.

Forty-odd years on, people are increasingly questioning those cherished institutions which were supposed to solve many such issues. For just as the European Community came to be associated with the rise in prosperity with which it coincided and to which it has undoubtedly contributed, it is now being held partly to blame for the economic malaise that is dampening people's faith in further economic integration.

The rot was already setting in well before the most recent moves towards further European integration. As Europe put the finishing touches to the Single Market and began preparing the way for Economic and Monetary Union, a cyclical downturn was already gathering pace across the continent, striking at different times and with varying degrees in each country. In addition, there was mounting evidence of structural handicaps in many of Europe's traditional industries, as well as in agriculture, making reforms harder and costlier on jobs than was envisaged. Europe's ageing population, together with other demographic changes, lay like a time-bomb beneath the generous welfare provisions across the Union, ticking ever more loudly in the early 1990s. International capital markets grew bigger and more volatile, while the seemingly recession-proof economies of South-east Asia undermined European industry's confidence in ever competing again.

This malaise gave birth to a new and energetic readiness to blame Brussels for Europe's economic ills. The European Commission, by trying to roll twelve sets of market rules into one, was accused of adding a thirteenth merely in order to satisfy its own thirst for power. As European Commissioner in charge of competition policy from 1988 to 1992, I was regularly accused of free-trade fundamentalism for cracking down on state aid when it was abundantly clear that governments were subsidizing some of their biggest companies further out of the world market, not back into it. They were just creating an industrial dependency culture.

The furious debate over Maastricht quickly overlapped with the completion of the Single Market, with Maastricht taking much of the blame for some of the less popular measures needed for that market. Opinion polls in Ireland, France and Denmark showed that voters were ready to attack Maastricht for issues which had nothing to do with it, nor even in some cases with the EU at all. Anti-Maastricht campaigners rallied support for their cause by denouncing farm reform, the Single Market, and even abortion. And they nearly succeeded, for the Single Market and other developments that preceded Maastricht were actually beginning to bite.

Once completed, the Single Market was to be Europe's crowning economic achievement since post-war integration began, but before the final building blocks were in place, the recession made it look tarnished in the eyes of those it was designed to serve. Nobody had doubted that the construction of such a market would be painful, but it still had the support of Euro-enthusiasts and sceptics alike, because it was conceived when Europe felt bold enough to trade in the short-term effects for the long-term benefits to the European economy as a whole. Recession has ushered in fear and a yearning for protection, despite the overwhelming evidence that protectionism will only put off the pain until another day.

It was not only the European Union whose reputation suffered as a result. National governments in Europe and well beyond grew increasingly unpopular. Voters vented their frustration by throwing out governments that had become tarred with the recession, unless the opposition was particularly weak or divided. The crushing victory of the opposition in the French elections in March 1993 is a case in point. In Italy the collapse of confidence went well beyond the government of the day, undermining the whole political system; and that confidence was ebbing away long before the full scale of corruption began rising to the surface.

The psychological impact has run deeper still, undermining confidence in areas of domestic policy that are normally shielded from the direct effects of the economic downturn. In Britain, the police and the legal system have come under fierce attack, while Germany's traditional open-door policy on asylum-seekers has been severely criticized. Educational standards and values have been thrown into question in several countries too, not to mention the role of the monarchy. A malaise as deep-seated as this one is a political fact of the greatest importance whatever its origin or justification.

The European Union, however, must itself take the blame for some of the adverse reactions to recent developments within it. The Community misread public enthusiasm for European unity in the 1980s and was tempted to wander into some areas where national or regional governments can legislate quite adequately for themselves. Its reputation as an overweening bureaucracy is greatly exaggerated, but it may not be *wholly* unjustified.

Knowing when to stop, therefore, is crucial if the Union is to carry public opinion behind it. That can only be achieved once Europe's governments have decided where the boundaries lie between what they do together and what they do alone. It will still be difficult even then, as those boundaries will be shifting all the time. That is why the future debate over finding the best level at which to take decisions, or 'subsidiarity', could be instrumental in cementing the Union's future credibility.

In essence, European nations should only act together where this will produce more satisfactory results than if they had acted alone. Take the environment. Nobody doubts that air pollution has no respect for national borders. Nor do they doubt that if one company faces less stringent pollution controls than its competitors abroad, it has a competitive headstart. It is reasonable, therefore, to expect EU member countries to decide such matters at European level. But it is harder to argue that the quality of tap water, whilst lamentable in some corners of Europe, constitutes a competitive handicap and hinders trade across borders. This is not an assault on environmental rules themselves but on the wisdom of the EU making all of them collectively. You can feel passionately about the environment and still believe in the right of national or regional governments to look after the purely 'national' or 'regional' aspects of it.

Sometimes the Union causes a storm by treading unwittingly on cherished national traditions which slip through unnoticed by the draftsmen. Europe is now perceived, wrongly, as a threat to hallowed French cheeses, German sausages and British savoury snacks, not to mention the linguistic accents on Spanish typewriters. When the offending provisions are spotted they are usually withdrawn, but by then the damage to the Union's credibility is done. Far better to find out more thoroughly in advance whether a new law will have an adverse, unintended or disproportionate impact before proposing it.

While it may have seemed natural in the past to let the Union legislate where possible, today there is no excuse for it to legislate except where strictly necessary. None the less, despite the Union's own excesses, its governments themselves are often to blame. There are times, for example, when draft EU laws grow too complicated because governments do not trust each other enough to allow a far simpler version through. The Union is usually blamed for these too.

Sometimes governments insist on rules that the Commission considers unnecessary, as was the case when the Commission reluctantly proposed a directive harmonizing safety standards for motor cycle stands.

One of the finer examples of governments overregulating themselves unnecessarily through Europe occurred when, as

European Commissioner for financial services, I steered through new rules on the trading of stocks and shares. Numbingly technical though the EU's so-called 'Investment Services Directive' may seem, it regulates an industry which is of vital importance to the European economy. The aim was clear: to boost business on stock markets by enabling brokers to trade company shares wherever and however they chose in the European Union, while ensuring adequate protection for investors. The original draft was simple enough, but it soon became an ideological football between the 'liberal' North and the 'protectionist' South, lying stuck for two years over a disagreement on stock market secrecy. France, Italy and others feared the North would scoop the trade off all the screens from Paris to Milan, bankrupting their stock exchanges through secretive marketing methods; and Britain, Holland and Germany felt some of their brokers would go to the wall if forced to publish trading prices earlier and more often, as the South demanded. Only by introducing a welter of detailed rules, provisions and let-outs was it possible to resolve the deadlock. The end result was a highly interventionist, if still worthwhile, piece of legislation.

Hunting down the culprit for every gaffe attributed to the Union is ultimately a fruitless exercise. The 'Union' as a whole will go on bearing the responsibility until ordinary people grasp the fine distinction between the role of the Brussels Commission and that of the ministers they themselves have elected. That is probably a tall order, but it does not lessen the need to explain far more clearly to those the Union purports to serve why the Union acts as it does.

Many farmers, for example, think that the recent reform of the Common Agricultural Policy is being introduced simply to do them out of a living. And yet farmers were leaving the land in droves *before* the CAP reform, whose central aim is to support the livelihood of farmers directly rather than rewarding them for producing too much at the European taxpayer's expense. Just how well has this been explained?

Excessive interventionism and inadequate explanation are the Union's own contributions to Europe's current malaise. To cure that malaise, we must take a sober look at the fundamental objectives on which the founding fathers built the Union. Their aim was to secure political stability and economic advance without trampling on national identity. They spoke of their intention 'to substitute for age-old rivalries the merging of their essential interests'.* It is by focusing on the essential and by avoiding the peripheral that we can restore faith in the Union.

Equally, there is a risk that we will be as blinded by the current mood of depression as we were by the euphoria that came before it. If in their anxiety to appease public opinion Europe's leaders cut the Union back too far, they could risk seriously undermining the stability on which Europe's postwar prosperity is founded. That is why now more than ever before Europe must remind itself that the Community it created has scored some considerable successes. If it had not, the aspiring members from Central and Eastern Europe, with their bitter experience of artificial union, would not be so keen to join; nor would some of those from Scandinavia, which have proved quite capable of prospering outside the Community.

It is equally misguided to believe that the Union can stand still without undermining its existing achievements. This is not infatuation for some ill-defined European ideal. It is firmly rooted in pragmatism. Most recently, the currency crisis of August 1993 has shown that the Union will need to pursue a degree of further integration if it is to survive. If

* This appears in the preamble to the Treaty establishing the European Coal and Steel Community, the precursor to the EC itself, signed by the six founding nations.

governments are left to handle their own currencies in isolation with no effective agreed common disciplines over monetary and economic policy, they will look to subsidies, trade barriers, capital controls and other insidious protectionist devices to keep their economies afloat. This in turn would stifle the Single Market, and we would be heading back to where we started.

In recent years we have spent too long arguing about the powers and responsibilities of the Union without focusing enough on the direction in which they should be used. The balance between the national ministers, national parliaments, the European Parliament and the European Commission is crucial, and I shall be exploring ways of adapting that balance to accommodate new countries as and when they join the Union. But it is the way we use those institutions that matters most.

We will only restore confidence by reassessing where nations stand in the EU, where the EU stands in Europe and where Europe stands in the world. That task must begin with the most exhaustive attempt to ensure that Europe takes decisions at the right level of authority, European or national. Once all the cogs of the EU's decision-making machine are well-oiled and turning together, Europe as a whole will be more effective in promoting the policies it wants on the world stage. We must work gradually towards freer trade throughout the continent, both East and West, while avoiding a clash between trade and other policies, notably the environment. And we must promote those same free trade principles more vigorously on the international stage, not through the use of force, threatening to close our markets unless others open theirs; but by dint of example, riveting our own barrier-free market firmly into place and seeking to mould world trade policy to its image.

It is clear that when we do proceed down the road, the

outlook for the European Union can improve very quickly, both economically and politically. Bringing the GATT Uruguay Round to a successful conclusion last year was a dramatic case in point. It immediately injected a much-needed dose of confidence into the European economy, as well as holding out the prospects of much greater prosperity, more growth and more jobs, when the trade barriers start to come tumbling down.

Reaching that GATT agreement was also of great political importance as it involved a healthy learning process within the European Union. The member states were forced to come together to reach a common position vis-à-vis the rest of the world. The British, for example, had to learn that French concerns about farming and the invasion of American culture were genuine ones that could not be ignored. The French for their part had to accept that the belief of Britain and other countries in breaking down trade barriers was not just the expression of some dogmatic ideology or a naïve reluctance to stand up to the Americans. It was, rather, a justified assessment that as the greatest trading bloc in the world Europe had most to gain from lowering trade barriers, and the most to lose from a new downward spiral of protectionist measures.

This process of coming together and showing a united front was as beneficial internally as it was crucial externally. It is fair to ask the Euro-sceptics: what kind of a deal do you think even the most powerful European country would have got if it had to stand up on its own to the United States, Japan and the rest of the world? And if greatly enhanced strength is achieved by working as one in trade negotiations, may there not be other areas in today's tough world where the same is true?

The revived unity of the European Union resulting from the long and difficult process of resolving its negotiating position in the Uruguay Round came across most dramatically at the end of the Round, when the Council of Ministers was able to decide unanimously and rapidly to accept the final outcome – indeed they did so a few hours before the negotiations in Geneva were formally concluded.

The importance of the signal given by that decision should not be underestimated. It was the first really major strategic decision taken by the European Union after the Maastricht Treaty came into effect: a decision pointing Europe firmly in the direction of a liberal trade policy and away from protectionism.

The outcome of the Uruguay Round and the restored unity that it imparted to the European Union certainly helped to lift some of the pall of disillusion and uncertainty that had hung over Europe for so long. But it could not in itself be sufficient to dispel the doubts and the gloom. To do that the other problems facing us need addressing in an open, honest and practical way.

If, for example, Europe is to exploit more open world markets to the full, governments must jointly develop domestic policies that give European industry the suppleness to fight against awesome competition abroad, notably from South-east Asia, while regenerating jobs at home.

As Europe's security needs cease to be identical in every case to those of America, Europe must shoulder more responsibility within NATO and outside it for its own defence through the gradual construction of a joint foreign and security policy, adapting to the post-Cold War climate without alienating its transatlantic partners.

And Europe must restore its battered faith in further economic and monetary integration, standing back from the recent currency turmoil and assessing what it has taught us about how we should move forward. The goal of Monetary Union remains one that is very widely shared, even if the Union is uncertain over how to approach it, so its governments must find a more flexible but equally determined path towards a single currency.

These are among the themes that I shall be discussing in the following chapters. The agenda is huge, but not impossible, if only the Union can organize itself efficiently. There is no need whatsoever for the recent controversies to cast us into despondency, but at the same time let us not forget that no civilization is guaranteed immortality. European values deserve to survive, but if the unification of Europe founders, ours would not be the first deserving cause to fail. We will continue to flourish only if we respond with vigour and imagination to the challenges we face. It is time now to buckle down to the task and show that we still have what it takes to succeed.

CHAPTER 2

What Should the Union Do?

Since the war, Western Europe has been striving to build the most solid safeguard against hegemony ever attempted throughout the bloody history of the continent. It is supremely ironic that the results of such an endeavour should be reviled as an assault on the cherished identities of Europe's diverse peoples. And yet reviled those efforts are, and the European Union which is carrying them out has suffered a loss of credibility as a result. Many people fear their nationhood is being sucked away and replaced by a grey, rootless Euro-personality. Europe was a fine idea when it meant the common market, many believe, but now it is gnawing at the core of their identity and should be curbed.

It would be easy to dismiss this fear as one of the many side-effects of recession. The EU's short history shows, after all, that enthusiasm for European integration wanes when unemployment is high and the economy is depressed. That is part of it, of course, but it is not all. This fear that the EU is roller-coasting people's identity into oblivion must be treated with the utmost seriousness, however unfocused much of the criticism may be. For it is on our handling of this question above all others that future generations will judge the European Union.

How great is the actual threat to the rich diversity of Europe's nations? It is clearly exaggerated. Not even the most Orwellian of minds could envisage Danish giving way to some amorphous Euro-speak (or even English) as the main language heard on the streets of Copenhagen; or Germans drinking their beer warm by the pint; or the streets of Milan and Athens full of businessmen wearing identical grey suits all cut to new Euro-standards. History, geography, anthropology, food and the weather have all made Europeans unshakeably different. Brussels has neither the intention nor the power to roll them into a single race, culture or nation. Travelling the 2,000 miles from the Aran Islands to Sicily or from Copenhagen to Seville will reveal a greater breadth of cultural diversity than anywhere else in the world. That, I believe, will never fundamentally change.

The Maastricht debate has brought these fears bubbling back to the surface. During the run-up to the Danish referendum on the Maastricht Treaty in June 1992, many Danes genuinely feared that their culture and traditions were disappearing. This reignited phobias about the encroaching Union that had surfaced as early as the 1970s. The larger and more tightly knit the Union became, the more they would be subsumed by their larger neighbours. Denmark would be dominated economically by the Germans and linguistically by the English. And yet the Danes were already among the most proficient English speakers in Europe, well before Maastricht, and their economy has depended heavily on trade and investment from Germany for many years, leaving them on average better off than their German neighbours. Europe's peoples *are* moving closer together, not because Brussels says so but because they travel faster, communicate more easily and do more business with each other. This is Europe's majority response to an ever more interdependent world, not a minority lust to defy history and turn Europe into a single country.

But it does beg the crucial question: what do European nations need to decide together, and what can they still do alone, in order to survive and thrive in such a world? The search for a flexible but lasting answer will take centre-stage in the European Union's development for the foreseeable future, all the more so as new countries join. Europe's leaders will succeed in that quest only if they follow four guiding principles – subsidiarity, democracy, tolerance and fidelity to the fundamental purpose of the Union.

Subsidiarity

Some say subsidiarity originated in a papal encyclical in 1930, some attribute it to Proudhon, while others go as far back as Aristotle. Whoever first coined the phrase cannot lay exclusive claim to the concept, however, for it has its roots firmly embedded in common sense and good government. As the English philosopher John Stuart Mill put it, 'it is but a small part of the public business of a country which can be well done or safely attempted by the central authorities'.

No sooner was it dusted down from the papal archives than the 'S-word' became a mascot for Euro-sceptics and enthusiasts alike, both using it to champion their vision of European integration. Both claims fall wide of the mark: subsidiarity does not mean rolling back the frontiers of European legislation, nor is it a new, politically correct euphemism for Euro-federalism. It is the search for the 'best level' of government at which to take decisions. It is not a static principle, for it should allow for the ebb and flow of responsibilities between regional, national and European authorities according to the need for Europeans to act alone or together at any particular time.

If followed correctly, however, it should stop the Union legislating for the sake of it, as the burden of proof would fall on those arguing for decisions to be taken at EU level. If a government, or indeed the European Commission, wishes to make a case for new Europe-wide rules on matters as diverse as pollution, worker safety, the financial protection of investors, or speed limits on motorways, it must argue convincingly that the individual efforts of each nation are not enough to protect Europe's common interests.

To meet this objective, the Union's institutions and governments should screen all draft Union decisions to test whether they could not be taken just as effectively by national or regional authorities. And since some people do not think it would be sufficiently objective for the Union's own institutions to carry out the 'subsidiarity check' properly, I will be suggesting in Chapter 9 that members of parliament, both national and European, should assume a key role in this task. Of course, even if the proposals survive this initial screening they will still have to go through the normal legislative process before they become law. They will still only become law if the vast majority of countries want that to happen. The screening will ensure that excessively burdensome and unnecessary proposals never even reach the starting line.

Existing EU rules should also be scrutinized, and if they fail the subsidiarity test, they should be delivered back into the hands of the governments that first agreed them. The Union should not set its laws in stone for ever, nor treat existing ones as sacrosanct. Some may clearly have served their purpose, while national governments may since have developed adequate powers and experience to perform the same task just as well themselves.

Deciding where this has happened is not going to be easy, and the Union may need to retain its powers for a long time in certain cases. Take Europe's 'anti-trust' policy, which obliges companies to compete fairly in the market place, for example. If companies were at liberty to monopolize markets and drive smaller competitors out of business, and if excessive government subsidies went unchecked, Europe's Single Market would become like a sports match without a referee. The Treaty of Rome gives the European Commission the power to ensure that all companies and governments play by the rules of fair competition, and to punish those who violate them. Without such powers, Europe's Single Market would begin to fray. The need to referee Europe's level playing field from a central vantage point, in this case the European Commission, will remain crucial until three key conditions evolve: firstly, when Europe develops a common business 'culture' with similar attitudes towards companies' ties with each other and with the state; secondly, when governments trust each other's curbs on subsidies and illegal business behaviour; and thirdly, when European governments write and enforce their own competition rules along Union lines. Germany and Britain have the most advanced rules, while France is catching up fast. Spain and Italy have yet to enforce adequately the competition powers they have, and many others have few provisions and even fewer teeth with which to enforce them.

If and when these three conditions were met, the Brussels Commission could begin to step back, gradually farming out the enforcement of competition rules to governments and national courts. But it should not happen a moment earlier; where there is business there will be no peace in the market place without strong competition rules to enforce it, for companies are driven by profit, not altruism. So long as there is one Single Market but twelve different views on how to regulate it, the Commission must remain the central arbiter. As the market matures and governments adopt the same national rules, the Commission can begin to hand over the reins, but not a moment before. The Commission itself never has nor ought to have the last word. Its decisions can always be challenged in the European Court of Justice.

As some powers ebb away back to European governments, others will have to flow to the centre, enabling those governments to tackle common issues better together than separately. Take monetary policy, for example. Germany's central bank is duty-bound to take only the needs of the German economy into account, even though its European partners often have to shadow German interest rates to avoid massive selling of their currencies. If a European central bank takes control of Europe's monetary policies, Germany's partners would sit round the same table as the Bundesbank, fixing interest rates to suit all Union countries, not just one.

Rigorous respect for subsidiarity will produce a more moderate, flexible and pragmatic Union, responding to the task in hand without tilting Europe towards any particular ideology. This in turn will reassure those who fear that European union is a one-way street towards a US-style Euro-government, with power gravitating inexorably towards the centre. Likewise, it will calm the fears of those who see Europe slipping back into a series of staunchly independent nations with little but a market in common.

Subsidiarity should not only put the onus on those who favour intervention by the EU to show why this is desirable; it must also be weighted in favour of the least restrictive form of regulation. The burden of proof should not just be on the centralizer, but on the regulator as well: if an informal agreement will do, then you do not need a law, or in EU terms, why make a Directive if a Recommendation is sufficient? Take the control of unfair advertising in cross-border tele-sales programmes, for example. This is a justifiable target for the EU's attentions as broadcasters in one country often aim their productions specifically at an audience in another, but each country has its own system of controlling advertising – which it cannot apply to broadcasts from outside its own territory. The first reaction was to draft the rules in tight and detailed format, but moderation prevailed, and the Commission eventually put forward a loose framework of legislation, though combining it with a very clear code of practice for the tele-sales industry, inviting them to regulate themselves. Only if this does not work will it be right to review the possibility of tying everything down in law. Common rules, if needed at all, should use the lightest form of instrument available, and avoid binding legislation where possible.

But is subsidiarity not merely a cloak which will still permit federalism in disguise, rolling the continent towards a United States of Europe? Far from it. It will leave Europe's governments far more power than the states in any of the world's current federations.

All federations have a constitution, which provides for similar government structures at all levels. Neither the Treaty of Rome nor the Treaty of Maastricht amount to any such thing. The Union's only powers are those bestowed upon it by its member governments, which are inclined to keep that power in their own hands unless they see an overwhelming need to pool it with their European partners. Centralization is the exception rather than the rule in Europe. Any attempt to force Europe into a truly federal mould would produce an unworkable mix of different executive, judicial and legislative cultures. For to compare the governments of Britain, Germany and Greece is to compare chalk with cheese. Not only do they differ in structure and outlook; they also preside over radically different models of regional government in each of their territories.

In a federation, the central administration tends to be structured like an octopus, with branches throughout the states which bring it close to all the nation's citizens, while answering to the government's central authority as well. There is no such structure in the European Union. Nor is there a coherent structure for the systematic redistribution of money from the richer to the poorer parts of the Union, which tends to be another hallmark of a true federation. Europe does have the so-called Structural Funds, for assisting the development of the poorer regions, but not systematically and organically devised as a way of redistributing money on the basis of regularly reviewed entitlements. The European 'Cohesion Fund' has a similar purpose, but here there is a very specific defined purpose: to help groom poorer nations for the tough monetary policies required in the run-up to a currency union.

If existing federations are anything to go by, Europe is neither on nor approaching the road towards federalism. The European nation state is too strong, too varied in character, and too rooted in history to be likely to conform to any of the federal models currently on offer.

Subsidiarity is now a pillar of European policy, enshrined for the first time in treaty form at Maastricht.* In fact, it has effectively been in force ever since, well before the Treaty's long-delayed ratification in October 1993 gave it formal legal weight. The number of new laws proposed by the European Commission has dropped dramatically, even as early as the second half of 1992. More importantly, the nature of those proposals has changed. In 1989, for example, there were ninety-two major legislative proposals; in 1994, about half that number emerged, and many of those merely update existing laws, and are therefore not major at all. Some of the Commission departments, Environment for instance, were chafing at the bit by the end of 1992 in the hope that the legislative wheel that ground almost to a halt after the Danish referendum could begin to roll as normal when the seventeen new commissioners set to work in the New Year. Instead, the new Commission insisted on shelving all but the most essential and least constraining proposals.

* Article 3b of the Maastricht Treaty reads: '. . . In areas which do not fall within its exclusive competence, the Community shall take action, in accordance with the principle of subsidiarity, only if and in so far as the objectives of the proposed action cannot be sufficiently achieved by the Member States and can therefore, by reason of the scale or effects of the proposed action, be better achieved by the Community. Any action by the Community shall not go beyond what is necessary to achieve the objectives of this Treaty.'

Of all policy areas, the environment is the one which best illustrates some of the potholes along the road to subsidiarity. Of course our environment is far too precious to be deprived of the most effective controls, but if set at the wrong level by the wrong authorities they risk being counterproductive. We have to avoid succumbing to a centralizing logic, a distorted perspective in which everything would be better done at Union level simply because that way we could be sure it would be 'right'. Every government minister knows the strong temptation to *do good*, but the Union may only define that 'goodness' for Europe's citizens when no lower level of government is in a position to do so.

There are local environmental matters where the Union *need* not intervene, leaving local authorities, for example, to grant planning permission for roads, buildings and other local development, and to manage forests and parks. And there are those global issues where even the Union *cannot* intervene adequately alone, for example to halt the depletion of the ozone layer or the disappearance of migratory birds. Here action at global level is needed if it is to be truly effective.

Between the two lie those pollution problems which European nations should tackle together. For example, acid rain from the heavy industries of Germany, France and the UK harms forests throughout Europe. Only common curbs on the emission of noxious gases can control such pollution without giving companies in some countries a headstart over others. Some forms of pollution will affect an even smaller group of countries, requiring even stricter cooperation between them: Switzerland, Germany, France and Holland tip industrial, nuclear and agricultural waste into the Rhine, clogging up the port of Rotterdam and damaging the North Sea. They now cooperate through the Rhine Commission to keep the river clean; but when everyone upstream of Holland dumps their waste and damages Dutch farms, the Dutch have no comeback other than through the European Union itself; the EU's 'common' moves against pollution can stop Germany's chemical effluent or the potassium salt from disused Alsatian mines, while the purely 'intergovernmental' Rhine Commission cannot. But both bodies can fruitfully co-exist the one within the other.

Other problems will spill over to the EU's neighbours: Eastern Europe needs our advice, and our markets, if it is to produce curbs as tough as our own to clean up the smokestack industries that churn fumes right across the continent. And we share a common interest with North Africa, the Near East and Turkey in keeping the Mediterranean clean, not least for the tourism on which many of its communities depend.

The search for the best level of government at which to decide a given issue is more likely to succeed if the Union adheres to an existing distinction between the hard and soft core of the EU's work. When the European Community was founded, its member countries chose to pool their responsibilities and create common policies on key issues so as to ensure the smooth functioning of the Single Market when trade barriers finally fell. They agreed to legislate together, and not individually, specifically in order to create one market in which people, goods, services and capital can circulate freely; they pledged to stick to one set of rules when trading with the outside world, and to one set of competition rules when trading with each other; and they organized their agricultural markets together, as well as agreeing in 1972 on a common regime to conserve fish stocks in European waters. Union countries must continue to legislate as one bloc on these hard core issues to make sure that the Single Market is firmly riveted in place.

Since then, successive European governments have followed the tide of events by deciding unanimously that additional policies need joint action, for nothing new happens in the Union without universal consent. But these are soft core issues, which need far more flexible handling. Very often European action is needed, but action involving purely voluntary participation is enough to do the trick.

Take the question of student exchanges, for example. Until the end of the 1980s, French, German and British students enhanced their studies with exchanges at each other's universities, but few other countries followed suit. The language and other educational facilities shared within this 'golden triangle' were of such high quality that few students were encouraged to branch out into other European nations, despite the ever-pressing need for greater training in Spanish, Italian and other languages as the Single Market gathered pace. Nor was there easy access to other nationalities outside that charmed circle. Consequently the ERASMUS programme was launched in 1987 to fund exchanges between all EU countries. The most enthusiastic response to this programme has come not from the golden triangle but from the others. Over half the Union's universities have chosen to join this *voluntary* programme, whose success has spawned similar link-ups with Eastern Europe through the TEMPUS programme.

Take the question of industrial research, too. The European Union offers funding, as well as databases, conferences and other tools to exchange information, in order to encourage companies and academic bodies to pool their research and development, avoiding wasteful overlap and building the competitive base European industry needs if it is to beat America and Japan to the technologies of the future. If the EU forced Europeans to share their research, the quality would suffer, even if cross-cooperation looked impressive on paper, for researchers alone can decide how to pick their partners.

Even voluntary actions of this kind need to be kept under constant review. In areas where the Union is not obliged by its founding Treaty of Rome to act together, subsidiarity demands that we review joint European initiatives to check that their value has not diminished. In ten years' time, for example, ERASMUS might become the victim of its own success, forging such close links between universities that they send students to each other of their own accord without needing 'marriage guidance' from ERASMUS.

Inevitably, the Union must keep deciding the most fundamental 'hard core' matters collectively until its governments trust each other's willingness, and ability, to police their common market with equal force. Governments perpetually accuse each other of bending the rules or failing to enforce them altogether, generating considerable mistrust among themselves, for which the Union itself is often the scapegoat. Some countries are indeed very much worse at obeying EU rules than others, a problem which could conceivably peter out as the Single Market slots gradually into place, so long as the EU Commission continues to beat the drum relentlessly. But it would be irresponsible to assure that this will happen. In the meantime, the banner of subsidiarity must not become a fresh excuse for governments to pick and choose which rules to keep and which to scrap; it means agreeing *together* which rules to keep, soften or drop, and which to enforce separately.

Equally, there is a risk of some countries enforcing Union rules with excessive zeal, and this can backfire. The case of toys in the United Kingdom shows just how easily this can happen. The Union has fixed a simple set of safety standards for toys, to avoid causing harm to children and to stop safety becoming a pretext for one country to discriminate against toys from a foreign producer. Parents who buy a teddy bear with the 'E' mark can thus rest assured it will be safe. Europe chose only to regulate new toys, as Europeans tend not to buy and sell second-hand toys across borders; but Britain failed to differentiate between new and second-hand toys bearing the 'E' sign, provoking an outcry from Oxfam and other charities, the bulk of whose toys became illegal overnight. Charities have lost business, while angry parents react by accusing the Union of interfering on an issue where the national authorities, not Brussels, are clearly to blame.

If subsidiarity is to become a genuine brake on excessive centralization, then the governments which endorsed it at Maastricht must take the main responsibility for seeing that it is applied properly. How can this be done? In some cases it is fairly clear: if the European Commission wants to propose introducing equal speed limits on all European motorways, it must convince governments beyond all reasonable doubt that their Single Market will run less smoothly without such limits. But if one government objects to the EU setting common axle sizes for trucks, where detailed Euro-laws already exist, will it have to prove by itself that it could set adequate standards alone without impeding the flow of foreign lorries on its roads? Or should the twelve governments have to provide collective proof before retrieving the right to fix truck sizes by themselves? And if ministers want the EU to acquire new powers, must they prove such powers are indispensable, or merely preferable?

A decision can, of course, be challenged in the European Court of Justice, but how will the Court react? Will it not shy away from taking the decision itself, arguing that something so political is the stuff of governments themselves? I believe the Court will leave the decision where it stands in the normal decision-making and only decide that subsidiarity applies to render proposed legislation unacceptable, if it would be unreasonable to come to any other decision. That is precisely the test that English courts apply to decide whether a discretion vested in a public body has been improperly exercised.

Democracy

Institutions, like objects in the dark, seem all the more frightening the less they are understood. Some of the best knocking copy against the European Union has come from detractors who variously describe it as undemocratic, bureaucratic, opaque and incomprehensible. All these labels bear a measure of truth, but the last two are perhaps the most apt; many of the European Union's current troubles would begin to fade if only a little more light were shed on some of the obscurer corners of the Union's decision-making machine.

Many believe Europe has a democratic 'deficit' primarily because they cannot discern the way the Union's democracy works for them. A deficit undoubtedly exists, and that is why European leaders sought to boost the powers of the European Parliament substantially in the Maastricht Treaty. But observe the misguided nature of popular dissent: the European Commission, accurately portrayed as 'unelected', is inaccurately accused of interfering, when no legislation can be passed except by ministers from national governments. The Commission can propose, but not take the ultimate decision. People believe, too, that EU rules are bounced undemocratically upon their governments at the eleventh hour; but most have been under the microscope of ministers' officials in numerous EU working groups for months beforehand, so much so that national parliaments hardly give them so much as a passing glance. Many of those who bemoan the shortfall in democracy also level against the European Parliament, Europe's directly elected assembly, accusations of waste, concluding that it should be curbed, not improved.

Europe has the means of considerable democratic expression, but it neither uses it nor explains it thoroughly enough. There are two main reasons. First, with the exception of Denmark, and to a lesser extent Britain, national parliaments do not scrutinize forthcoming Union rules closely enough, and appear to have little influence on their ministers when they travel to Europe to decide those laws amongst each other in the Council of Ministers. Secondly, the EU is its own worst public relations enemy, for it makes little effort to explain itself to those it purports to serve.

Europe has made several stabs at improving its image in recent years; but bold promises of more openness by European leaders at their Birmingham and Edinburgh summits in 1992 have had little follow-up.

The rule-making procedures themselves are opaque, and need exposure to far more vigorous public scrutiny. The Commission should comb industry more thoroughly for its views, through greater and earlier use of Green and White Papers before introducing proposals for legislation. For example, the Commission produced in July 1992 a proposal on timeshare properties in order to stop consumers from taking snap decisions which they later regret. Six months later, Europe's heads of state agreed that this was the kind of thing better left to governments themselves. Would it not have been wiser to sound out the terrain first with a Green Paper?

The European Union's paperwork, too, is incomprehensible to all but a few experts and the authors themselves. Few of those who draft it are writing in their own language. Of the Commission's administrative staff, only a third or so have English or French as their mother tongue; yet these are the only two languages in which texts are drafted. Even fewer staff have everyday readers in mind when drafting, as they should. In addition, the paperwork needs better codification. Attempting to understand a draft EU law is like a paperchase, as one amendment refers you back to another, then on to another, eventually leading you to the original, which by then has changed beyond all recognition. Ministers have updated some pieces of legislation almost every year. For example, Directive 85/3/EEC, defining weights and dimensions for road vehicles, was adopted early in 1985, amended in 1986, 1988, three times in 1989, and again in 1991 and 1992. How much easier it would be if they wrapped all new amendments up into a new, legally binding text at regular intervals. Codifying laws that way might be tedious work, but it would give the uninitiated the chance to grasp the essence of any draft, and how it has evolved, just by reading it once. Which is why, at the end of 1993, the Commission proposed a new and codified text on road vehicles, sweeping all these amendments away.

Europe also needs a 'Freedom of Information Act' laying out generous conditions under which the public could view documents. This would ruffle feathers within the Union's institutions, for many EU officials fear their vital contacts in industry and elsewhere would withhold information if confidentiality were lifted. To reassure them, the Act could insist on the Union gaining prior approval from the supplier before publishing any information classified as confidential. People are thirsty for information, and justifiably so, about EU laws which will affect their lives. And yet many documents are withheld unnecessarily through lack of a coherent information policy, making leaks a daily occurrence. An Information Act would make the Union's institutions open by design, rather than by default as at present.

The Union needs to work harder to explain itself, and to equip others to do so on its behalf. Children learn at school about the governments, parliaments, police, local councils and other institutions that run their society, but the European link is frequently missing from the chain. Businessmen often live in partial ignorance about European Union rules, vaguely aware of their importance but unable to work out how to obey them, exploit them or even seek to change them if they are interfering unnecessarily with their particular line of business. Glossy brochures and whistle-stop lecture tours around the provinces by EU experts will not suffice. The European Union and its governments must encourage schools, youth organizations, chambers of commerce, environmental groups, charities and other bodies to fill out the education gap on Europe. They must not proselytize or resort to propaganda of any sort; Europe is neither a movement, nor a belief, nor an ideology. It is a piece of public property to which people have rightful access in order to equip it with the rules which best suit the needs of their society.

Tolerance

The closer Europe's profoundly different peoples draw to each other, the more visible any discrimination between them will be, and the more vigilant they must become to avoid it. The draftsmen of the Treaty of Rome foresaw this, and wrote quite plainly, in Article 7, that 'Within the scope of this Treaty . . . any discrimination on grounds of nationality shall be prohibited'. And yet even the most dictatorial of regimes always pay lip-service to tolerance, promising not to discriminate on grounds of religion, race, sex, age or colour. What difference will a small mention in the Treaty of Rome make to reassure people who fear that as the countries of the continent converge, the big fish will swallow the minnows, and the protection of the vulnerable few will give way to the promotion of powerful business interests?

If the European Union is to live up to its pledge of non-discrimination, it must pursue tolerance with vigour. Tolerance must be an active, not a passive quality, with the Union moving swiftly within its powers to keep European integration from treading on national or cultural identity; but it must also show restraint. The Union's role is to prevent discrimination that could harm the business that its member governments have decided to share, notably the Single Market. The Union will retain credibility by stamping out discrimination 'within the scope of this Treaty', and not beyond. That scope may increase as more seemingly domestic issues take on an international dimension; but the EU must always act as a cross-border policeman and not a local bobby. It may show force when patrolling its beat, but it must not step beyond it.

Governments have assigned their Union the task of ensuring equal pay for men and women. Article 119 of the Treaty of Rome demands that 'Each Member State shall . . . ensure and subsequently maintain the application of the principle that men and women should receive equal pay for equal work'. Once enshrined in law, all simple principles like this one are swamped by case law, explaining, interpreting and elaborating; but the substance is relatively straightforward: sex discrimination is illegal in Europe when it comes to pay.

But why does the EU not outlaw sex discrimination altogether, not just on salaries? Because pay affects cross-border business, and while the Union remains economic in nature, it must limit its policing to cross-border trade and anything that may hinder it. Pay is a major determinant in industrial competition between countries: if women suffer discrimination in their private lives, in their leisure time or in their ability to find housing, their government should justly intervene. The Union should even encourage it to do so. But employers who systematically pay women less than men could gain an unfair headstart over their competitors elsewhere in Europe, and the Union itself should therefore step in. Far from turning a blind eye, Europe would then be handling its rightful powers responsibly.

The EU's founders had the foresight to identify the threat which sexual discrimination could pose to the construction of their Union, but they would have to have been clairvoyants to predict the extent of today's racial tensions. Europe's leaders should act swiftly to outlaw racial discrimination in broadly the same way: by a simple addition to the Treaty of Rome, they could make it unlawful for employers to discriminate in ways that invariably leave those of different colour or ethnic origin in lower-paid jobs. At their next intergovernmental conference, they should insert something along the lines of: 'Member States shall ensure that discrimination as to pay on grounds of racial difference shall be illegal. For the purposes of this article, "pay" shall be defined as under Art. 119'.

But why stick to racial discrimination on pay? Is not racism a hydra which needs slaying whenever it rears one of its many ugly heads? Surely Europe needs one protective umbrella to cover its Welshmen, Catalans, Jamaicans, North Africans, Poles and other races, nationalities and ethnic communities. Without it, who is to say the Sikhs would be as well recognized and protected in Germany as they are in Britain, where the Sikh community is strong, or vice versa for Turks in the UK? The answer lies, once again, in the European Union acting firmly and decisively, but only within its appointed role. Racial discrimination is illegal in all EU countries, usually through their constitution, and legal definitions of race exist in all states. The EU must stamp out racism where it threatens economic life between those countries, while urging them forcefully to stamp it out themselves on their own domestic ground. If racism is on the rise, it must be stifled at all levels of government, and the EU should seek to reinforce, not smother, the national struggle against it. The Union should not seek to do it all, but what it does, it should do well.

The closer knit the national policies of the members of the Union become, the more effective the campaign against racism and other human rights abuse will be. Europe can help dovetail those policies by encouraging all governments to write the European Convention on Human Rights into their national lawbooks. All EU states have signed it, and individual people can appeal to the European Court of Human Rights in Strasbourg if they feel that a judgement from the national courts still does not respect their grievance adequately.

But to reach this stage, citizens currently have to exhaust all options under their own national legal system, including appealing to the highest courts in the land. If the rights which the Convention lays down were actually incorporated into national law, citizens could seek that same protection directly through their own national courts, since it would form part of their own national law. This would be quicker, easier and cheaper for everyone. A disaffected citizen in search of justice at European level can head for the European Court, but, as with a game of croquet, only after passing through all the hoops and hurdles of the national courts on the way. How much easier it would be to be able to get the national court to give its own view at the outset.

Sticking to the core principles as Europe evolves

The European Union has not always carried public opinion with it as it evolves, partly because many suspect it of deceit. No sooner, it is alleged, are we told to accept the blueprint for a Single Market than its leaders start pushing for full monetary union, leading to a further loss of 'sovereignty', a single currency. And as people are struggling to digest that mouthful, talk of 'political union' appears as though out of thin air. 'That's not what we signed up to', goes the refrain among those who suspect an increasingly centralized European state of creeping up behind them, as though the integration of Europe were a game of grandmother's footsteps.

This allegation can be answered by carefully tracing who said what, when, but there remains a lingering suspicion of a lack of complete candour. Europe's leaders should bear the main responsibility of explaining their message and their further aspirations openly to their citizens. A Single Market, for example, makes more sense if it is accompanied by a single currency and if its rules are scrutinized more closely by directly elected Euro-MPs, a key element of the 'political union'. These are legitimate goals which stem from the Union's original tasks, among them the creation of a common market. But the depth of public concern carries a serious warning: Europe must change only by building on its original foundations; if it moves site altogether, people will conclude that their worst fears are being confirmed. And that means preserving the primacy of the nation state and the identity of its peoples without reducing their capacity for effective joint action in areas where they have chosen to converge. The balance is an extremely delicate one, which we disturb at our peril.

The Maastricht debate has seen some countries gaining the right to 'opt out' of parts of the process, while encouraging talk of others pushing for closer union and creating a 'multi-speed' or 'two-tier' Europe in their wake. This is Europe's new vocabulary of change, causing much wringing of hands and implying that if all members do not march in step, some will fall irretrievably behind. The men who founded the Union, far from turning in their graves, would see it as quite normal, for there is nothing new in some European member countries wishing to push ahead faster than others, either in groups or alone. Belgium and Luxembourg fused their currencies even before the Treaty of Rome was signed; and together with the Netherlands, they chose to drop customs barriers ahead of their EU partners. Nine of the present Union members, frustrated at Europe's persistent failure to secure the free movement of its people, are removing border checks between themselves through the Schengen Convention. Far from undermining the Union, they have the blessing of the European Commission and Parliament.

There is a danger that as some countries forge their own

tighter links, they will already have set the mould by the time the late-comers catch up. Indeed, many believe Britain's late entry into the Union explains its current reticence towards further European integration, for the British suspect that the model on which it is being built serves Franco–German interests better than their own. Britain and Ireland risk suffering the same sense of lost influence, though to a lesser extent, if they join the Schengen agreement as late-comers in several years' time. Whenever such a situation seems looming it is right to focus the argument in Britain (and elsewhere) on whether it is better to join now despite all the inadequacies, or risk being left behind and being forced to join later on a less satisfactory basis.

Since Britain decided to opt out of the additional social provisions of the Maastricht Treaty, some of the country's biggest firms have expressed the belief that Britain will eventually join its eleven partners, but too late in the day, by which time the rules that shape some of the social issues facing the Union will already have been written. This is thoroughly unpersuasive. Europe has now entered a period of reflection following a spate of legislation on social affairs. In 1989, eleven member countries adopted the Social Charter, then fleshed it out with an Action Plan of some fifty specific measures including rules on working time, the protection of pregnant women, and the employment of children and adolescents. Most are agreed, or are well advanced in the legislative pipeline. The cogs of the social policy wheel have since slowed down, giving way to a more reflective mood. Indeed, in November 1993 the European Commission adopted a Green Paper on social policy, inviting reflection and comment about what, if anything, the EU should now be doing.

Britain's fellow Union countries are less likely to push through a rash of social laws now that they know that the UK will no longer be there to block them, but will not be bound by them. Moreover, Europe is currently gripped more by the need to discover how its social system may be handicapping its efforts to compete against America and Asia than by a desire to tighten the belt of social protection around its industry.

As the Union expands, its component parts will tug increasingly hard in different directions. Soon it will have to abandon its *ad hoc* approach to countries wishing to integrate further and faster than others, and replace it with something altogether more systematic. Two alternatives face the Union: either it accommodates those countries wishing to opt out temporarily from policy areas as diverse as Economic and Monetary Union, foreign and security policy, and social and home affairs, paving the way for a hard core of nations to forge ahead; or it drops the cherished right of its members to veto new steps towards integration, allowing changes to the Treaty of Rome to come into force once ratified, say, by 80 per cent of European countries.

The former path may seem fraught with dangers, risking a certain degree of disunity, but the latter is wholly unacceptable to governments, at least for the foreseeable future. Smaller countries would justifiably resist it as a threat to their very existence, while it would also be bitterly opposed by the Euro-sceptics even in Europe's bigger countries, and give them a legitimate stick with which to beat the Union. There is no third option. Opting out, therefore, is here to stay, and Europe has simply got to learn to live with it.

The Union, then, is not going to become an all-pervading octopus. Subsidiarity has rightly come to stay. Properly applied it will prevent unnecessary and obtrusive intervention in national affairs, while permitting the Union to take on new tasks on behalf of its members, which it alone can perform. At the same time the Union is likely to be a less tidy, less uniform organization. It is our task to ensure that this can be, and be regarded as, a sign of flexibility, rather than an indication that the Union has been so amorphous as to be enfeebled as a result.

CHAPTER 3

Economic and Monetary Union:
The End of a Dream?

Many would have us believe that 1993 was the year in which the European dream was shattered in the currency markets. Integrationists, they say, had seized on the short burst of economic growth in the 1980s to turn Europe into a creed. With scant regard for the nuts and bolts of sound economic management, they whipped up political fervour for ever-closer ties between radically different economies, spreading the gospel of a single currency by firing up citizens and their leaders with the metaphors of movement. Never mind 2,000 years of sovereign diversity, Europe was now reduced to a bicycle: you pedal it forward or fall from the saddle; or a train, whose guards were impatiently calling all passengers aboard for Monetary Union; or an unstoppable tide or current; or merely a series of stepping stones, leading Europe across the stagnant waters of separation towards the verdant pastures of Economic and Monetary Union.

It failed, they say, because Europe made the fatal mistake of putting politics before economics. The single currency was an artificial construct invented by the Euro-enthusiasts as the main motor for integration, but it would never have worked, for common sense and national interest would inevitably triumph in the end. The lumbering beast was already tiring when recession and German reunification hunted it down and brought it to its knees, leaving the currency speculators to scavenge over the remains. Now that the beast is dead, they say, Europe can focus on the issues which matter most:

reducing unemployment and spreading the gospel of free trade.

However, it would be a serious economic and political misjudgement to assume that the currency crises of 1992 and 1993 mean that Europe should never have a currency union, or that it will never want one again. The turmoil that struck Europe's Exchange Rate Mechanism was not inevitable. It was the product of an unfortunate cocktail of recession mixed with the sudden, painful fusion of the two Germanies. Moreover, in no way does the ERM crisis weaken the case for Economic and Monetary Union in Europe: a system of closely linked exchange rates and a single currency are two quite different animals.

Far from being an artificial political construct, a single currency would be a natural complement to the European Single Market. It could also help Europe address the acute unemployment and flagging performance currently afflicting its industry, even though such goals are sometimes portrayed as unrelated to a single currency. And there is no reason why the outline for an Economic and Monetary Union sketched out in the Maastricht Treaty should no longer be valid. Yet there can be no doubt that Europe's currency crisis has rocked it severely, forcing us to look again at the path along which Maastricht proposed to lead Europe the full way to a single currency. Ironically, the crisis could be a blessing in disguise, giving governments the chance to align the running and performance of their economies more closely so that if and when a single currency arrives, it will stick.

Why did the ERM hit the rocks?

Before discussing how it should develop in the future, it is worth assessing the ERM's history and performance to date. Europe is not alone in seeking stability between its currencies, nor is this a particularly new trend. Throughout most of the twentieth century, the major world economies have sought to reduce fluctuations in their exchange rates. First through the Gold Standard, which pegged currencies to the price of gold until the 1930s, and later through the Bretton Woods system which pegged currencies at a fixed rate to the dollar. Both these systems ushered in long periods of stable exchange rates, fuelling growth and enabling countries to open their markets wider to each other. Small wonder, then, that in Europe, where trade and economic interdependence were deeper than anywhere else in the world, the Union should have sought a replacement for Bretton Woods after it collapsed under the weight of the oil crisis in 1973.

After some early experimentation with fixed but movable exchange rates in a system known as the 'snake', Europe launched its Exchange Rate Mechanism in 1979. Its initial membership of eight countries swelled over the next decade, and by 1992 all EU currencies except Greece had joined. Other countries with close economic links, such as Austria, Sweden and Finland, also linked their currencies with varying degrees of closeness to it. The ERM works by setting central exchange rates for each of the participating currencies, against an artificial European currency known as the 'ecu'. The ecu is an average of all currencies participating in the system, weighted according to the strength of each economy and thus the solidity of its currency. The agreed central rates against this composite currency are then the focal point around which the national currencies may fluctuate. Under the original two-band system, strong currencies could only dip above or below their central ecu rates by up to 2.25 per cent either side, rising to 6 per cent either way for weaker currencies. If any currency strayed outside its band, the central banks of participating countries would have to intervene, buying in from the money markets if the exchange rate dipped below the band or selling if it rose above it. If a currency bounced stubbornly along the ERM floor despite such intervention, its central rate could be realigned.

By and large, several currencies would rally round their floundering partner by realigning up or down marginally rather than allowing the one to fall heavily on its own – it was in their own interest to do so to prevent any one country from gaining a sharp competitive edge over the others by devaluing its money. ERM members thus tended to cooperate rather than compete with their currencies. The early years of the ERM up to the mid-1980s were punctuated with small, collective realignments, which did not hinder the considerable degree of monetary stability as a result of which cross-border trade in Europe flourished faster than at any other period since the Community began.

Currency stability in Europe, as predicted, boosted trade, investment and consumption. But the ERM also brought more general improvements in economic management. It imposed greater discipline on governments' handling of public spending and the money supply, spreading lower inflation across all ERM countries, thanks to the key role played in the system by the Deutschmark. The Deutschmark is Europe's strongest and most stable currency, and thus has the greatest weight in the ecu basket as the anchor of the system. Its reputation stems from the discipline and independence of the body that runs it: sealed off from interference by politicians prepared to debase the currency in order to ease pressure on the public purse, pay back debts or gain votes, the Bundesbank became the standard-bearer of sound monetary discipline. Its Governing Council is constitutionally bound to stabilize prices, and the impact of this commitment was vividly illustrated in the mid-1980s when German inflation hovered around 0 per cent while it reached an average of 3 to 4 per cent in the rest of Europe. By lashing their moorings to the German currency through the ecu which it dominated, other

ERM members restricted themselves to three choices: they could either bring inflation down to German levels so as to keep the credibility of their central ERM exchange rate; or they could let their currencies become overvalued, losing export markets as a result; or finally, they could devalue, raising import costs and thus risking an upsurge of inflation in the economy.

In the 1970s, many ERM members had chosen to blend some inflationary discipline with a slow but regular weakening of their currencies against the Deutschmark, but during the 1980s, the world began to develop a different collective view of macroeconomic policy. The long-standing orthodoxy that running higher inflation rates would help to bring down unemployment began to wither, encouraging governments to focus on curbing inflation as the central target of their monetary policies. As a result, ERM countries grew more willing to fight inflation by overvaluation, holding their exchange rates constant and exorcizing price increases from their economies by exposing them to the full force of competitive prices in Germany.

Price discipline soon spread to workers and employers who realized that if they pushed for higher wages they would lose their ability to compete, and with it they would lose markets and jobs. With inflation running at 10 per cent and interest rates at 15 per cent, Britain joined the ERM in 1990 to benefit from this swift and well tested remedy. British inflation promptly fell to 3.6 per cent by August 1992, allowing interest rates to be cut to 9 per cent. By the time Britain joined, the ERM had won its spurs, forcing countries to approximate the management of their economies and generate prosperity together. In some member countries, economic management changed out of all recognition in the new ERM. Both France and Ireland, for example, had until the mid-1980s traditionally been high-inflation countries. But throughout the 1980s they both acquired a reputation for being committed to low inflation through their membership of the ERM and the credibility which they gradually built up for their ability to resist the political temptation of easy money and growing public deficits. These successes encouraged Europe to entertain the serious prospect of taking an ambitious step further down the same road by creating a single currency.

In their zeal to secure stable exchange rates through the ERM, as they did so successfully from 1987 to 1992, its members in fact failed to operate the ERM as its founders had intended. One of those founders, former German Chancellor Helmut Schmidt, made this clear when Britain was forced out of the system in September 1992. The ERM, he explained in a radio interview for the BBC, was never intended to be a fixed rate system. It was always intended that there should be a realignment of exchange rates if the pressure upwards or downwards on a currency was so great that it could not be stopped by central bank intervention in the markets, or could only be stopped by changes in interest rates of an extent altogether unsuitable or damaging to the economy concerned. Instead, governments had resisted realignments at all cost, in the mistaken belief that such realignments could be altogether avoided, and that this was the best way to move to a single currency.

Nevertheless, this appeared not to matter in the late 1980s and early 1990s, for ERM members seemed to be successful in tracking German monetary policy very closely, shadowing cuts and rises in key German interest rates almost instantly, and avoiding forced devaluations as a result. In practice they had surrendered their independence over interest rates to Germany, although legally it remained in their hands. While Germany and its partners shared the same economic needs – stable prices, sound spending policies and low inflation – it made sense to keep aligning currencies closer together. Had those needs not diverged drastically, monetary union might have stayed on course.

But the shock of German reunification drove a wedge between the economic performance of Germany and its ERM partners. West Germany effectively bought up the East German economy overnight, and the cost far outstripped even the most alarming estimates. Its near-worthless currency abandoned for the Deutschmark, East Germany relied totally on Western subsidies to bring its roads, telephones, pollution standards and industrial performance up to Western levels. Pensioners could no longer survive unless paid in Deutschmarks, while the soaring cost of unemployment hit the Finance Ministry in Bonn as workers were laid off on an unprecedented scale in order to pull the industries of the old East around.

In 1990, private-sector German forecasts put the bill for reunification at 115 billion Deutschmarks between 1990 and 1994, or about 25 billion Deutschmarks per year. But by mid-1993, estimates of the cost from 1994 onwards had risen to 65 billion Deutschmarks.* The impact of reunification on German monetary policy was immense: forced to borrow massively to shore up the East and facing a resurgence of inflation – by then a species driven to the brink of extinction – Germany was confronted with a stark choice: either raise taxes to pay the costs or hike up interest rates. The government argued that it was politically impossible to raise taxes enough to absorb reunification costs; that left the Bundesbank with little option but to raise interest rates, and the rest of Europe felt the pain.

* This includes the special fund set up to pay for German unity, as well as the costs of servicing old East German debts and other transfers, but it does not include the costs or assets of the Treuhandanstalt, which privatizes former state-run firms in the East.

Europe could have gritted its teeth and endured high interest rates under normal circumstances. After all, reunification was a European as well as a German goal, so it was only natural to spread the cost. Europe, however, was in the throes of a severe recession. In 1992 economic growth tailed off, and in 1993 it fell by 1 per cent. And after financial deregulation had led in the late 1980s to a boom in lending and spending, the money-lending industry returned from the party with a stinging hangover of debt. Governments as well as private citizens had worked up massive overdrafts. In Italy and Belgium debt stocks soared to over 100 per cent of GDP, while in relatively cost-conscious Britain real personal disposable incomes fell for the first time in over a decade under the burden of accumulated debt. Dawn broke over the 1990s and the party ended, leaving governments, consumers and business cautious about spending again until their income brought their debt to within more sustainable levels. This caution held back any chance of a recovery from the recession, forcing governments to cut interest rates as deeply and swiftly as possible so as to entice business into borrowing once again and jump-start the economy. German interest rates, however, made this well nigh impossible.

Europe's economies needed radically different remedies to cope with recession, debt or the cost of reunification. If this provided the tinder, it was political uncertainty over the future of the Maastricht Treaty which produced the spark that ignited speculation against European exchange rates. Denmark rejected the Treaty in June 1992, spreading doubt and fuelling further speculation through the summer. As opinion polls became too close to call shortly before the French referendum on the same Treaty, speculators began trading on the likelihood of Europe diverging away from a single currency, rather than converging gradually upon it as Maastricht had foreseen. Once Italy devalued the lira early in

September, the dealers realized they faced a one-way bet on currencies overvalued against the Deutschmark, as well as on those whose governments thirsted desperately for lower interest rates either because of their debt overhang or because of high unemployment and low economic activity.

Speculators began bombarding all vulnerable currencies, whether devaluation-prone or not. Given that sums the size of the UK's annual GDP can be traded on international foreign exchange markets in any one day, governments could do little to resist speculative pressures. Later in September, sterling and the lira left the system rather than accept a forced devaluation within it. Waves of attack against other soft targets, notably the Danish kroner, the Spanish peseta and the Irish punt, continued into 1993, showing no clemency despite the sound economic performance of all three countries. Three general realignments took place between September 1992 and May 1993, in addition to bilateral changes between currencies. The seemingly stable health of the ERM was finally beginning to deteriorate.

Economics and finance ministers and the governors of Europe's central banks fussed over the patient, studying whether its sickness stemmed from flaws in its very anatomy. They prescribed no fundamental changes, concluding simply that the system should be run as initially intended, with currency realignments taking place whenever necessary.

This set the scene for a battle over the future of monetary and exchange rate cooperation in Europe. France desperately needed lower interest rates to stimulate recovery and tackle unemployment, perhaps the key issue that brought crippling defeat to the Socialist government in the legislative elections. And yet despite this, French interest rates continued to shadow German rate movements very closely. The credibility of the ERM seemed to have come to rest on an immutable Franco–German exchange rate parity. For it was this fixed parity which had turned the franc into one of Europe's strongest currencies, giving France lower inflation and a healthier current account than even Germany's. Although France attempted to capitalize on the economic progress it had made by cutting rates faster than in Germany, the markets were wary of such arguments. Once clear signals emerged that Germany would not cut its own rates in the near future, France could not resist the pressure of speculation without the politically unacceptable decision to raise interest rates. Soon the franc became a one-way bet, staving off devaluation on the strength of political will alone. It bounced along the ERM floor, trading below it on more than one occasion. As any damage to the currency relationship would break the ERM irreparably apart, first officials then ministers held crisis talks to discuss how to save both.

At pains to avoid the impression that the ERM was finished, they loosened it as far as possible without breaking it: ministers agreed to stretch the degree of permitted fluctuation from 2.25 per cent to 15 per cent either side of the central parity. This sent two signals, one economic and the other political: it gave currencies more undergrowth in which to hide from speculators, who could no longer assume governments would realign exchange rates if they needed to cut interest rates; and it was hoped that observers of European integration would be reassured that the ERM was alive and recuperating. On the down side, however, there was a risk that such wide fluctuation margins could prompt a return to exchange rate instability and high inflation, both of which would damage trade and economic recovery in Europe. It looked, therefore, like just a temporary solution.

The ERM has undeniably been damaged by the turbulence of 1992 and 1993; but it would be foolhardy to talk of the ERM's demise, and more foolish still to assume that it has taken all prospect of Economic and Monetary Union down with it. Critics wrongly portray EMU as a larger, more awesome version of the ERM beast. It is in fact a different species altogether. For under the ERM, no matter how fixed politicians want them to seem, exchange rates can still change, giving the speculators a target. EMU would remove the target altogether, fixing parities permanently and creating a single currency. It would also prevent governments from running their own conflicting monetary policies, whether on purpose or by default, for the European Central Bank would run the single currency. The ERM crisis, therefore, tells us little about the workability of a single currency, nor does it diminish the case for one, which, there is every reason to believe, would produce positive benefits which would go well beyond the benefits of the ERM.

The case for a single currency

Critics assail EMU as yesterday's cure for yesterday's ailment, namely inflation. Today, they argue, real interest rates have risen so high that the key target of Europe's economic and monetary policy must be to cut unemployment and restore industry's ability to compete. There is a fear that EMU could actually exacerbate these problems.

This is grossly misleading, for a single currency could in fact alleviate both. Cutting costs is a major component of competitiveness, and European businesses suffer the cost handicap of currency fluctuations, which neither their American nor Japanese counterparts have to face. These form a significant commercial and psychological barrier to decisions on what to produce and what to consume.

To begin with, the costs of converting from one European currency to another can themselves be prohibitively high: the Commission has estimated that Europe's companies and citizens would save as much as 15 billion ecu a year, or nearly

0.5 per cent of the Union's entire GDP, with one currency instead of twelve. Moreover, the smaller Union countries with less internationally recognized currencies will reap much of the benefit, as will small and medium-sized companies for which transactions in foreign currencies can prove cripplingly expensive. Evidence shows that the transaction costs of maintaining different currencies can strip a company of about 15 per cent of the profit it makes on sales in other European countries. These costs are considerably greater for small and medium-sized firms.*

Secondly, separate currencies act as a psychological barrier to companies considering business abroad. The creation of the European Single Market has encouraged managers to take the plunge and invest elsewhere in Europe rather than take the more comfortable option of trading just at home; but currency costs dampen their enthusiasm for branching out into foreign markets, particularly during recession. The Union can go some way to overriding these fears by making Europe's financial system more competitive, trimming banks' high margins when dealing abroad and slimming down the time it takes and the price it costs to shift money across borders. But the psychological barrier will remain so long as the currency hurdle persists.

Thirdly, a single currency would reduce the risk that impairs a company's ability to plan for the longer term. As long as there are separate currencies there will be a risk of exchange rate fluctuations, and as long as rates change, companies cannot predict their future profits with any reasonable degree of accuracy. The ERM held this at bay by holding its members to within the $+/-2.25$ per cent fluctuation bands. Companies can, of course, 'hedge' their currency risks,

* For more details of the Commission's work on the costs and benefits of a single currency see 'European Economy, October 1990 – "One Market, One Money"'.

insuring against future fluctuations and adapting their strategy as a result, but once again this favours large companies which can afford to run a treasury management team to manage its finances in today's complicated world of international currency, futures and options markets. Preliminary estimates by the Commission suggest that even only a small reduction in the risk premium of currency changes could raise income by between 5 and 10 per cent in the long run as companies invest more and boost growth. So the end goal of a single currency would be the natural complement to a Single Market in which companies plan where to invest and sell on a Union-wide basis.

Attaining the goal will yield the most immediate and obvious benefits, but even the path leading to that goal could also deliver substantial macroeconomic gains. The path towards EMU requires European states to cut excessive public spending if they are to groom themselves for currency union. This will help rid them of inflation, which tends to stunt growth, boost unemployment and reduce a country's per capita income. Governments will no longer be allowed to borrow and spend more than their economy can support if they are to join the monetary union, and these constraints will in turn reinforce the climate of stability.

A single currency will also give Europe greater political clout in the international monetary system, giving European countries more control over world monetary decisions than they currently exercise with their separate currencies. The ecu will emerge as the third monetary pillar alongside the dollar and the yen, greatly strengthening Europe's voice in international policy coordination. With a single currency, Europe would have a more powerful voice in calling for a world monetary regime which contributes to, rather than cuts across, an open international trading system. In recent years when there has been no system of exchange rate cooperation, major trading nations have frequently accused each other of deliberately undermining their currencies in order to gain a competitive edge in export markets and they have in turn used this as a justification for erecting trade barriers or other restrictions against each other.

The case for a single currency is then as strong as ever, but does the Maastricht Treaty still offer the most appropriate way to achieve it?

There was a clear assumption until August 1993 that Europe would advance gradually towards a currency union as prescribed in Maastricht, with the ERM slowly but surely drawing the currencies together and cementing them finally into a single money for Europe. There would be no major changes in currency parities or in the shape of the ERM more generally, ahead of the final move towards a single currency; any preparation for that step would involve adapting and creating the right procedures and institutions for it, but not altering the ERM itself. The currency crisis challenged this assumption, forcing both some central rates to change and the loosening of the ERM bands so that the Union could ride out a tempestuous period of speculation during 1992 and 1993. The ERM is now a rather different vehicle taking us on an altered route to monetary union, but in spite of these changes, the crisis has in no way undermined the goal of EMU set out in the Treaty.

The Treaty of Maastricht establishes three coordinates for the move towards EMU – the timetable, the required number of countries to start the monetary union, and the qualifications for membership. These coordinates remain as robust as ever, despite the recent squalls on the money markets.

When? The timetable for EMU

The Treaty envisages three stages in the evolution towards a single currency. Under stage I, which never formally existed but in practical terms ran from 1990 to 1993, EC states abolished curbs on capital flowing between them, and were supposed to place their currencies within the narrow bands of the ERM. Speculation put an end to these narrow bands, but free movement of capital has remained in place, despite the temptation to re-introduce capital controls. Furthermore, the main element of stage II still went ahead: as of 1 January 1994, the Union established the European Monetary Institute that would gradually shed its skin and hatch the full European Central Bank.

On the face of it, and indeed until the 1993 crisis, stage II looked as if it would be purely procedural, but in fact it ushers in some fairly important policy innovations. First, central banks and finance ministries cooperate on a formal footing. Policy remains firmly in national hands, but they coordinate their control of exchange rates, spending and the monetary supply more closely in order to pave the way for the creation of a single central bank. Other economic policies are also coordinated more closely, thanks to the broad economic guidelines set down by the European Council in Brussels in December 1993, which established common priorities for European governments and a code of good economic practice. Moreover, under stage II, national central banks are supposed to move towards independence from governmental control, thereby increasing the credibility of their policies in the fight against inflation. Governments are also under an injunction to avoid overspending and running the public purse into deficit.

But stage III contains the most contentious provisions of all, namely the deadlines by which Maastricht envisages the arrival of a single currency. The Maastricht timetable for EMU has attracted the most criticism of all, both before and after the ERM crisis. Detractors argue that by setting artificial deadlines, the Union is frogmarching its governments into a single currency earlier than their peoples may wish and their economies may allow. There are two alternative starting dates – 1997 and 1999 – by which European countries could fuse their currencies into one, and the exact quorum rules for each are different: Maastricht states 1997 as the year when a single currency could come into being if a majority of member states were ready and willing to join. Two years later, the need for a majority of countries would lapse. Those who wish to proceed to stage III, no matter how few, would do so, provided they met the strict criteria laid down in the Maastricht Treaty.

And yet derided though they are, these deadlines are more realistic and less artificial than they may at first appear. Critics forget that EMU is not a one- or two-shot game in which the objective falls for ever if participants fail to meet it the first or second time around. If 1997 seems unrealistic now, let us not forget that only a couple of years ago that did not seem the case, and in a couple of years from now at least the 1999 target could easily once again seem a feasible one – certainly for a core of countries whose membership would be sufficient to make a single currency viable.

Furthermore, the Maastricht deadlines have a catalytic effect on governments, focusing their minds on the need to align the way they run their economies, even if they remain undecided about the final destination of a single currency. It is easy to put off difficult decisions if there is no obvious deadline, and no clear cost to the delay. The Treaty has presented governments with both the deadline and the cost, warning that they will be unable to participate, however good they may think they are as Europeans, unless they narrow the gap between the varying performance of their economies. No one wishes to be left out on the grounds of poor economic performance, and the Treaty has given governments a lever with which to make much needed but unpopular improvements to their economies, streamlining industry and reducing public spending in ways which hurt in the short term. In the case of Spain, for example, the drive to meet the conditions for a currency union has enabled the Spanish government to push through economic reforms that might otherwise have been politically unpalatable among its heavily unionized workforce. Equally, Ireland, and the Netherlands to a lesser extent, have begun to bring down the burden of national debt which had accumulated over many years in order to qualify for stage III. This means that in future they will be able to devote a lower proportion of national savings to repaying old loans and more to productive investment.

Who? The membership of the club

While the Treaty is tough on the economic disciplines required of countries before they join a single currency, and cajoles them along with persuasive deadlines, it has an open-door policy towards countries that consider joining. In this sense it is like a club with tough standards of behaviour and dress, a loose regime on opening and closing hours, and with no discrimination or favouritism towards its clientele. This is crucial, for the government leaders who signed the Treaty are fundamentally aware of two factors: first, that some of them may be ready and willing to form a single currency before others, and must not be stopped from doing so; and secondly that, in the long term, a single currency will work more effectively the more European nations join it.

Clearly the wider the membership of the club, the greater the potential benefits to all in terms of exchange rate stability, and the more powerful the single currency will be in influencing world exchange rates and global monetary policy. It is in the Union's interests, therefore, to achieve as broad a membership as possible, provided all participants meet the strict rules of admission. But this in turn must not stop some forging ahead when they are ready, so long as they do not create a permanent, hard core currency zone that will streak ahead of the others, making the latter's eventual membership harder and harder to achieve. A two-speed Europe may be inevitable, but it must not become a permanent two-tier Europe with an unbridgeable gap between one tier and the other.

In order to avoid a widening gulf between those aboard a single currency and those still unable to join, or those like Britain and Denmark with the right to think further before committing themselves, there must be tight currency collaboration. This will prove more necessary the more countries join; those governments which hold out against a single currency would, in theory at least, be in a position where they could exploit their national currency flexibility to give themselves a short-term competitive advantage over the others. Weighing against this temptation will be the familiar inflationary price of competitive depreciation and the Treaty commitment to treat national exchange rates as a 'matter of common interest'. These arguments suggest that stage II, which is now under way, could usefully be devoted to strengthening economic and monetary cooperation in ways that can continue even when some member states are able to proceed to a single currency.

How? The convergence criteria

Those who attack the single currency itself are equally scathing about the rules of admission, but without good reason. The Single Currency Club does not insist on its clients wearing outlandish garb unsuitable for anywhere other than the interior of the club itself; it requires clothing that is pretty uniform in style, but suitable for all weathers. In other words, the Maastricht Treaty demands that adherents to a single currency run economic and monetary policies based on sound common sense, and in step with one another. It demands policies that will lead European countries to prosperity anyway, with the added long-term bonus of a single currency if they succeed, but certainly no economic disaster if they do not.

What are these rules? Maastricht lays down four minimum conditions before countries can join an Economic and Monetary Union:

- Governments must not live beyond their means. Government deficits must not exceed 3 per cent of gross domestic product.
- Governments must not run up heavy debts. Maastricht decrees that government debt must not exceed 60 per cent of GDP.
- Inflation must be kept at bay, and must not exceed 1.5 per cent of the average inflation level prevailing in the three countries which are tackling inflation most successfully. This ensures that as countries align the way they manage their economies, they move gradually towards the inflation performance of the stronger economies.
- Likewise, long-term interest rates must not rise more than 2 per cent above those in the three countries which have best managed to keep interest rates down. This gives an indication of whether the markets believe that inflation rules will converge in future. If one country requires higher long-term interest rates than another, it is a clear sign that higher inflation is expected in that country.

The underlying objective of these criteria is to draw economies closer together so that when they decide in favour of a single currency, they will be resilient enough to withstand it. And yet the criteria have been accused of imposing rigorous disciplines so far removed from economic reality that they exclude countries from an eventual EMU rather than enticing them towards such a union. Experience shows this to be misguided. One might have thought after Britain's traumatic exit from the European Exchange Rate Mechanism that it would never wish to go anywhere near such disciplines again. Yet the British government adopted an indicative medium-term deficit target of 3 per cent of GDP – similar to the minimum target decreed by Maastricht – considering it to be consistent with sustainable economic growth, even during a bitter recession.

The importance of tackling debt, recognized in the 3 per cent and 60 per cent target figures, is significant, for governments and independent central banks have come to appreciate just how much high debts can threaten currency stability. The rocky period that shook the ERM has shown how governments and central banks alike can clamour for lower interest rates in order to grapple with excessive debt as much as to keep the currency stable. But these two Maastricht criteria still draw the most fire, notably because many countries particularly during the recent recession have moved further away from fulfilling them.

There is even a strand of opinion which believes that these criteria could do more harm than good. For is it sensible to stick to a 3 per cent government deficit target during both the depths of recession and the peak of the economic cycle? Is it reasonable to expect a country like the Netherlands, in which the money markets have implicit faith, and which is the only currency to have been able to maintain a 2.25 per cent link with the Deutschmark, to reduce its government debt to GDP ratio from its current level of 80 per cent to the Maastricht target of 60 per cent, at an undoubtedly high political and economic cost?

The answer to both these questions is yes. We would not wish to create a permanently deflationary situation by sticking to such targets through thick and thin. But only an incomplete reading of the Treaty would lead to these questions being raised, for the Treaty explicitly states that if a member state exceeds the 3 per cent government deficit criterion the Commission shall prepare a report which will take into account 'whether the government deficit exceeds government investment expenditure and take into account all other relevant factors, including the medium-term economic and budgetary position of the member state'. There is nothing to prevent a short-term deficit exceeding 3 per cent, provided that the economic reasoning underlying an increase over this medium-term target is sound. Equally, there is some room for flexibility over the government debt/GDP target. No one is going to prevent a country from joining the single currency if it fulfils all the other criteria and its debt to GDP ratio 'is diminishing and approaching the reference value at a satisfactory pace'. The Treaty will not in itself allow us to manage the transition to EMU on automatic pilot. A certain amount of discretion and common sense will be essential ingredients if the EMU recipe is to succeed.

The other two criteria have attracted less attention, because they are more obviously prerequisites of a single currency. In fact they may even surprise some people since they do not demand the complete harmonization of interest rates and inflation, only their concentration in a narrow range. It will be possible for inflation to vary by small amounts between different members of the monetary union, even after the move to stage III, because some components of the inflation rate, like housing costs and local transport, are specific to their local area.

Long-term interest rates must converge at a low level before the start of stage III, because this is an indication of how far low inflation policies are held to be credible. If one member state's long-term interest rate is considerably higher than another's, this is a sign that the markets generally do not believe that the first member state will be able to match the second in terms of inflation performance. Under these circumstances the markets will demand a higher interest rate if they are to invest money over a long period in the country with less credible anti-inflationary policies.

These two monetary criteria ensure not only that a monetary union is stable at the time of its inception but that it is likely to continue to be so for the foreseeable future.

Where does this leave us?

Over the last year or so, it has become fashionable to regard 1997 as a totally improbable date for stage III to begin. The smart money has even begun to question the feasibility of 1999. But this is to a large extent the inevitable result of two to three years of deep recession. Even today, at the bottom of the economic cycle, seven member states meet the inflation criterion and three others are very close. Equally, ten member states meet the long-term interest rate criterion, illustrating just how much inflation credibility has been won over the past five to ten years. Today only Ireland and Luxembourg would qualify under the strict 3 per cent rule on deficits, but five other member states including Germany, France, Denmark, the Netherlands and the UK are close to this and can expect to reach a 3 per cent target in the not too distant future or once the recession is over and their spending on unemployment benefit is reduced and tax receipts begin to rise with economic activity. Even the most problematic criterion, the debt/GDP ratio, does not look today as if it will be a bar to the single currency either in 1997 or 1999. Already, Germany, Spain, France, Luxembourg and the UK are under the 60 per cent threshold. Denmark, Ireland, the Netherlands and Portugal are either close or could well be allowed to qualify if they maintain current efforts to repay old debt. All in all, therefore, it is not beyond the bounds of possibility that a majority of member states will be ready in 1997. Barring unforeseen disaster, it is already clear that four or five core countries should be able to form a single currency in 1999.

Where next?

The goal of a single European currency remains as valid after the ERM crisis as it did before, and the desire for it has hardly diminished among most European countries. The first stage towards it as defined in the Maastricht Treaty has already arrived, and the prototype for a European Central Bank, as demanded by stage II, is now finding its feet. But if the currency turmoil has left the beginning and end of the process of Economic and Monetary Union intact, it has seriously undermined much that lies in between. Stage II will not be as straightforward as first imagined, and this might affect either the timing of a single currency or the initial membership of it. The crisis of August 1993 has left us with a 15 per cent currency band and a series of options as to how to proceed onwards from it. I believe member states can choose one of four paths:

1) They can allow their currencies to float temporarily until economic conditions improve and they choose to draw their exchange rates closer once again.
2) Some of them can take a sudden plunge into a currency union, outwitting the speculators and forcing participating governments to yield the management of their monetary policies to one single central bank overnight.
3) They can return to the narrow fluctuation bands of the ERM as it stood before the crisis, proceeding as before in the hope that burgeoning recovery and post-crisis caution will avoid a repeat occurring.
4) They can maintain the current wide bands while taking credible and sustainable steps to ensure that the perform-

ance of their economies starts to converge without facing pressure to align exchange rates beforehand. When they are close enough, the old currency straitjacket of the tight ERM bands will seem like a loose smock as they opt with relative ease for a single currency.

1: FLOATING CURRENCIES

Monetary stability is now so dear to the hearts of governments and central banks that no argument in favour of floating currencies free of all exchange rate discipline has gained ground in the debate over Europe's monetary future, however tempting such freedom might be. All governments whose currencies have either left the ERM or been flung to its very edges by the speculators are anxious to restore some control over their exchange rates and avoid undermining the years of work that have gone into creating the Single Market. The currency crisis has left governments no less responsible than before, even when tempted to let their currencies become undervalued in order to steal a march on their industrial competitors by selling exports more cheaply. This has just not happened.

2: TAKING THE PLUNGE INTO A SHOCK CURRENCY UNION

This alternative won a considerable following as the money markets picked mercilessly on one European currency after another. Many economists felt the best answer to the crisis lay in an instant fusion between the Deutschmark and three or four other 'inner core' currencies, forging an advance union of their own. This had strong appeal: it could secure the heart of Europe's future monetary cooperation, saving it from the voracious appetite of the speculators. After all, the economies of Germany, the Benelux countries, France and Denmark were already managed and performing so closely together that a single currency might seem little more than a short political step away. A shock union would by definition have stopped a run on the French and Belgian francs and the Danish kroner, but their widely differing economic needs would not have vanished overnight. Germany still needed to curb the inflationary pressures of reunification by keeping interest rates high, while the rest of Europe needed lower rates to climb out of recession. This option was looked at with interest, but ultimately not pursued.

3: RETURNING TO THE NARROW BANDS

A return to the good old days when the narrow bands of the ERM kept a buoyant Europe's inflation in check might seem attractive to those with a long-standing commitment to currency cooperation. It would certainly stop countries from out-devaluing each other in order to win over their competitors. But even the most ardent old-timers are forced to accept that narrow bands alone will not suffice to quell the speculators. A further defence would be needed to buttress currencies against the markets until a single currency was achieved. And yet every one of those buttresses on offer would emphatically do more harm than good: Europe could reintroduce controls on the free movement of capital, unearthing one of the cornerstones of the Single Market; or it could force currency traders to lay down a deposit or pay tax every time they bought foreign exchange, in order to stop them selling it quickly afterwards. Under this scenario, Europe's money would simply flow offshore unless all the world's financial centres imposed the same controls together. For all their gut appeal, neither of these options ever gained a large following.

4: KEEPING THE WIDER BANDS, BUT COOPERATING BETTER WITHIN THEM

Europe's currencies have been thrust apart by the currency traders, who capitalized on countries' diverging economic needs. The ERM owes its continued existence to a political decision to sustain it in a form so loose that speculators cannot predict government's monetary moves with any degree of certainty. That political decision, together with the failure to find serious fault with the ERM itself, strongly implies that Europe's governments intend to use the ERM as a vehicle for restoring closer monetary cooperation. Yet they also recognize the dangers of closing the gap between currencies before their economies themselves converge.

Europe should make a virtue out of the difficult situation thrust upon it. It should use this opportunity to take a more creative approach, responding to the changed economic climate. Freezing parities was perhaps a sensible approach for a period in which member states needed to convince themselves and the markets that they could and should bring down inflation, but the world has moved on now. We should no longer seek exchange rate stability as a means of forcing economic and monetary convergence. Instead there should be a Union-wide agreement on an inflation target backed up by an agreement to maximize the rate of monetary growth that can be permitted without jeopardizing the achievement of that target. Those countries which have not exceeded the agreed rate of monetary growth should be allowed to cut interest rates, even if it brings their exchange rate down.

This would allow those countries which have high interest rates, but which thirst for recovery, to cut their interest rates even if Germany does not. But I would stress that this will work or be acceptable to the member states only if it does not jeopardize their hard-won credibility as staunch fighters against inflation. That is why any moves in this direction must therefore be accompanied by a strengthening in cooperation or accepted criteria on which independent interest rate reductions could take place. The most appropriate and direct indicator is the growth of the money supply. If Europe has an agreed notion of what average European inflation and money expansion should be, it should encourage member states to seek the interest rates which are compatible with these overall objectives.

As a result, countries would be free to release interest rates from their moorings alongside Germany, but without provoking either inflation or competitive devaluation between currencies. The effect would be a revised pattern of exchange rate relationships, better reflecting economic needs, and a gradual move out of recession. In due course, when all currencies have shaken down to their appropriate levels, governments could decide at leisure whether or not to return to the narrow bands. Whether or not they do this, those countries eager to advance to a single currency could do so at the appropriate time by simply freezing their exchange rates where they stand. As they would already have achieved a high degree of convergence in the way they run their economies, the move to a single currency would still be politically painful, but economically effortless.

Conclusion

The most turbulent currency crisis in the short history of the European Union rapidly became a field-day for the I-told-you-so's. Like most upheavals which have rocked modern-day Europe to its foundations, this one brought pro- and anti-Europeans out of the woodwork, either proclaiming the death of Monetary Union or the ever greater need for it. The antis argued that you can never buck the markets, while the pros retorted that you can, and should, by imposing a single currency, for the money-changers will always upset stability until driven out of the temple altogether.

Both arguments have some validity. The speculators showed that any attempt to force the pace of Economic and

Monetary Union by squeezing currencies closer together before economies are ready could have the opposite effect; but this does not herald the end of Economic and Monetary Union altogether. Ministers and central bankers have shown their commitment to EMU by continuing to stick as closely as possible to the previously existent exchange rates, rather than use their new-found freedom. This may be laudable politically, but has not necessarily been wise economically.

If you cannot buck the markets but you want a single currency, what do you do? This is arguably the most important economic question that the European Union will have to answer in the coming years. The three-stage approach to Monetary Union laid out in the Maastricht Treaty is more flexible than its detractors would have us believe. But the deadlines of 1997 and 1999, by which first a majority and then a minority of states can forge a single currency, are in many ways the least important although the most talked about aspect of the move to a single currency. Much else in the Maastricht approach remains clearly valid: the 'convergence criteria' are based on economic common sense, and governments would be wise to follow them whether they still envisage a single currency or not.

Maastricht, therefore, is both useful and harmless: it promotes sound economic discipline and sets up the institutions that will eventually run a single currency, and if you stop assuming that the ERM means 'semi-fixed exchange rates', then Maastricht does not force European governments to attempt to freeze their currencies prematurely before their economies are ready. Yet this still leaves the crucial question: what do you do with currency rates while drawing the management and performance of Europe's varying economies closer together? I believe governments should exploit the newly stretched ERM to their advantage, dropping interest rates to boost recovery and letting their currencies slip if necessary, but only if their hold over the money supply gives them the leeway to do so without risking an upsurge in inflation. They should also agree to avoid undercutting each other's currencies while cooperating even more strictly than at present on how to align their economies.

With recovery in place and economic discipline sustained, a common currency will once again become a realistic goal. It is ironic that to ensure the effective construction of a single currency, currencies themselves may have to be the last building block to fall into place.

CHAPTER 4

Making Europe More Competitive

To an outsider watching the debate over Europe's weakening performance on the world economic stage, Europe might seem like a sinking ship whose officers, rather than bailing out the water and mending the leak, stand on deck bickering in nine different languages over what it was that punctured the hull. Is Europe losing the fight for world markets because its labour costs are too high, or are we just failing to train our staff properly for the future? Are governments too meddlesome in industrial affairs, or are they not intervening enough in order to channel companies and workers into the lucrative technologies of the future? And can we actually reverse the decline, or are we merely going the way of all civilizations, living over-luxuriously in the false security of past achievements as poorer countries overtake us?

If handled properly, the debate raging in Europe over the slipping competitiveness of its industry, far from increasing the damage, could hold the very key to its future prosperity. The ship *has* been taking in water, imperceptibly slowly, for many years. All of Europe's governments have prescribed their own national remedies, some with more persistence and therefore more success than others. But it has taken a long and bitter recession to galvanize Europe's governments finally into contemplating new thinking to combat industrial decline right across the European Union.

So far it is a fresh and inexperienced debate, fertile with new ideas or repackaged old ones, but far from clear on its ultimate conclusions. There is a risk, too, that it could become blurred by ideological discord, with some proponents blaming labour costs, others the short-sightedness of government; some lamenting the excess of state intervention, others the lack of state leadership. If Europe is to gear up its industry and services sector to the fight for future survival, it must put aside its ideological baggage and carry out the most detailed, rigorous and dispassionate analysis of what makes European industry tick, as well as what makes some sectors strong and others weak. This exercise must cover all aspects of Europe's macro- and micro-economic performance, including monetary policy, labour relations, management and training, technological research, market opening and the efficiency with which companies can raise capital. It will be a delicate balance: we need to produce a prescription tailored to improve the efficiency of the European economy without borrowing ill-fitting theories and practices from elsewhere, but without seeking an exclusively 'European' solution to Europe's ailments either. An answer must begin from the premise that Europe is growing ever more interdependent on its world partners; cut the European economy adrift in the hope of keeping it afloat, and Europe will spring an even bigger leak in its capacity to survive in an ever more competitive world. And eventually it would hit the rocks.

The European economy is run by governments of varying political hue, pushing different policies on labour, finance, investment and other central cogs in the economic machine. They differ in ideology and emphasis, and yet they are already beginning to outline a common diagnosis of Europe's industrial ailments. All European Union governments now maintain that high unemployment is caused partly by rigidity in Europe's labour markets. Almost all say the costs of employing low-skilled staff are too high for companies to bear. They broadly agree on the need to remove whatever dissuades firms from setting up new plants and factories and from taking on new workers. Moreover, they agree Europe must curb runaway public spending if its economies are to recover. They believe that insufficient capital investment, research and development, as well as a disjointed network of roads, telephone lines and other communications across the continent, are blunting Europe's competitive edge. And they agree that companies in the European market must improve the quantity and quality of their products while lowering costs. All believe this means training a more skilled workforce. To revive Europe's flagging economy, its companies must install a new 'quality culture' capable of producing new ideas and turning them rapidly into goods and services that create and win markets on a global scale.

Most Union member states also recognize the urgent need to open up new markets for their exporters. The trend is now heading more towards attracting customers with sophisticated, top-quality products and away from the use of brutal cost-cutting tactics to outmanoeuvre overseas competitors and gain market share. Many governments recognize, too, the vital need to encourage small and medium companies in order to stimulate economic growth and employment creation.

Europe is not alone in agonizing over the cause of its collective economic ills. The world recession has proved fertile soil for studies into the causes of economic malaise and the ingredients required to solve it. One such analysis from the World Economic Forum and the International Institute for Management Development in Lausanne outlines eight factors which can make an economy more or less competitive:

– The basic strength of the domestic economy, as a result of the effectiveness of macroeconomic policies.

- An economy's participation in trade beyond its own borders.
- The role government plays in making industry more competitive.
- The efficiency of the capital markets in helping companies to raise money, and the quality of banking and insurance in order to improve the business climate.
- The availability of good transport, communications and other infrastructure, enabling business to move raw materials to the factories and goods to the shelves fast and reliably.
- The efficiency with which managers make their companies innovative, profitable, responsible and forward-thinking.
- The existence of a sophisticated research system which spawns good ideas and enables industry to turn them into best-selling high-technology exports, securing a lead in world markets.
- The efficient use of people themselves, ensuring workers are well qualified and trained for the jobs that exist in a fast-changing economy.

The study claims that in order to grow into new markets and keep them, an economy must use its infrastructure, finance, technology and people (its so-called 'assets') as efficiently as possible; and it must improve its 'processes' – the quality of its goods, the speed of delivery, its adaptability to consumer demand and the service it offers.

This is useful analysis in itself. But how does Europe score against its chief competitors? Out of thirty-five leading economies surveyed, Japan beats all European partners in five of the eight categories, and most of Europe in the remaining three. The United States scores poorly on the treatment of staff and on the quality of its infrastructure. Europe emerges with mixed results: it does badly on training, research, management and in some cases on the strength of its domestic economy, while scoring higher on the quality of its financial management. The overall message is clear: European governments are still not providing business with the optimal range of policies most needed to boost their competitive ratings.

The deepest world recession since the Second World War has thrust a new economic realism on Europe. Consumers and producers alike have lost confidence in the future. Their leaders are unanimous on the need to act, and they even agree on much of the diagnosis. They must now convert this sense of gloom into a joint search for a common cure. If Europe fails, this would of course dishearten and alienate Europe's peoples still further, weakening the structure of the European Union itself. For the economy is the engine-room of Europe's integration. If it falters, people and business begin to lose their nerve, and that affects even Europe's cast-iron achievements, such as the unified market. Post-war political history has shown that Europe tends to come to a standstill when the economy is in a trough. And experience shows that the Union either moves forwards or backwards, but it hardly ever lies securely moored to its berth. We should be striving for what President Kennedy called 'a high tide to raise all ships . . .'.

What are the roots of Europe's economic malaise?

Despite the common perception of the 1980s as a period of sudden growth, Europe's economy did not instantly burst into song after decades of economic hibernation. The roots go far deeper. During the 1970s, Europe's economies were weakened by inflation and the rapid increase in oil prices, which drained away 1–2 per cent of European gross domestic product. During the 1980s, their performance picked up, enjoying far lower real prices for oil and other commodities, fast expansion of international trade, greatly reduced inflation and latterly more prudent handling of public finances, tax and the money supply.

Then came the creation of the European Single Market. The mere prospect of that market catalysed European business into thinking and planning on a European scale: in the long run-up to 1993, companies positioned themselves for trading in the world's biggest barrier-free market. This in turn triggered an upsurge in cross-border mergers and a race to create economies of scale to meet the demand from the 350 million-odd consumers shopping in that vast new market. Confidence soared and business soared with it. Comparison with the performance of our main competitors, however, takes the shine off Europe's economic success. The US, Japan and now the newly industrialized economies of South-east Asia are out-stripping European growth and the trend is worsening. The European Commission's economic growth forecasts (November 1993) point towards the dynamic Asian economies growing annually by between 6 and 7 per cent in the next few years — 5 per cent above expected growth rates in the European Union. The US economy is also growing faster than that of the EU. And as for Japan, its growth performance has outstripped our own in every year since 1986, a trend likely to continue in 1994 and 1995.

The fall of Communism signalled the victory of democracy and private initiative and stiffened the resolve of governments to pursue free market policies. It spurred Western governments to push on with privatization and market reform *despite* the economic downturn, particularly as the newly liberated economies of the East were swallowing free market principles, at least in theory, with an avidity rarely seen in the West. The reduction of state intervention has undoubtedly taken hold, even though the recession has bitten hard into unemployment, increasing resentment against government austerity. Europe grew steadily, but not spectacularly, through the 1980s, masking the underlying problems until the recession of the early 1990s forced awareness of them on the public consciousness.

Finding a diagnosis to the problem

In Europe we invest much less than in Japan, we consume a bigger slice of our GDP, and our governments spend 10–20 per cent more of GDP than do Japan or the United States. This implies that our savings ratios are too low to sustain enough investment. Nor do we export enough for our trade balance to offset these trends. The macroeconomic consequence is that our growth, whilst broadly matching that of the United States, has fallen dramatically behind that of Japan and the 'Tiger' economies of South-east Asia. Europe is also limping behind in the race for the world's lucrative high-technology markets.

The cost of unemployment

Together these factors have prevented us from creating new jobs in growing areas of the economy. In the late 1960s just 2.5 per cent of Europe's workforce were unemployed. This rose to 4 per cent in the 1970s, nearly 10 per cent on average during the 1980s, and there will be an estimated twenty million people out of work in the mid-1990s. The private sector, too, has been a sluggish creator of jobs, more so than the public sector, while quite the opposite occurred in Japan and the US. In Europe, private firms have brought between three and four million new jobs on stream since 1973, while the United States has created ten times more and Japan three times more over the same period:

	Net increase in employment 1970–90
USA	28·8 million
Japan	11·7 million
EU	8·8 million

Source: *Commission figures in its contribution to White Paper on Growth, Competitiveness and Employment, Dec. 1993.*)

In Europe, unemployment is particularly severe among unskilled workers, young people and women, a sure sign that the labour market is functioning poorly. By 1992, the ranks of the 'long-term unemployed' – those out of work for over a year – had swelled to almost 50 per cent of Europe's jobless and 17 per cent of our unemployed youth. Of that 50 per cent over half again have been on the dole for at least two years. To explain this away as a side-effect of a cyclical downturn in the economy is to do those people a serious injustice, because unemployment has risen through every business cycle in the last twenty years. Even if Europe's GDP were to grow by 3.5 per cent a year until the end of the century, the jobless total is unlikely to fall below 6 per cent.

What is causing this rigidity? Like a vehicle too heavy to turn corners sharply, Europe's labour market is not manoeuvring efficiently enough to redeploy large numbers of workers into burgeoning areas of economic growth. European employers have tended not to adjust salaries sufficiently flexibly in line with a worker's qualifications nor with the amount he or she produces and earns for the employer. The cost of labour in Europe is high, too, even without counting the salary itself, and workers receive insufficient training and retraining to keep their skills fresh or to give them new ones for new tasks. There is also excessive rigidity in working time, in the use of part-time jobs and the ability of companies to hire and fire. And it is crucial that governments should not tax people disproportionately while working, as this strips the jobless of incentives to seek work, thereby fostering 'unemployment traps' and lengthening Europe's long-term job queues even further.

It is a false and heartless view to think that unemployment merely lightens the burden of industry. It wastes a nation's potential wealth as well as rotting the fabric of society and throwing whole families into despair. It creates a working superclass and a jobless underclass; a Europe of two social speeds with an ever-widening gulf of alienation between them. The prospect of twenty million unemployed in the European Union is socially and economically unsustainable. The great political challenge for the European Union and its member states is to introduce policies that will significantly dent these unacceptable levels of unemployment, whilst maintaining the fabric of European society.

Europe's social security and health services are among the most admirable and generous in the world. They are also among the most costly to the public purse. European Union nations already spend twice as big a slice of GDP on welfare as Japan and 60 per cent more than the United States, forcing governments to levy high taxes to meet the cost. This can only grow worse, as Europeans live longer, driving up pension and health costs even further.

How well do Europe's companies perform in high technology?

Europe nurtures high-performing companies of its own as well as providing a fertile market for outside companies to expand, enriching the European economy in the process. Europe is still the most inventive continent of all, with more patents in the pipeline than either the US or Japan. The most recent data available, covering the 1985–9 period, shows the EC had a 38 per cent share of total inventions compared to 27 per cent for North America and 24.4 per cent for Japan. But this apparent lead hides the fact that European inventions cluster around engineering rather than in basic sciences, and are not always at the sharp end of technology. For example, European inventors lag behind the Americans in biotechnology, genetic engineering and advanced materials, and are way behind the Japanese in microelectronics.

Yet despite Europe's good ratings in the hit-parade of the world's most successful multinationals, a strong foothold in the lucrative technologies of tomorrow still seems to elude us. Europe is weak in electronics, communications and other aspects of information technology. In addition, companies accuse Europe's rule-makers of tip-toeing far too cautiously into the world of biotechnology, strangling new ideas and products with approval procedures far more cumbersome than those of our main US and Japanese competitors.

It is important to be aware of the size of the future markets at stake. The Commission's White Paper on Growth, Competitiveness and Employment forecasts that biotechnology will mushroom into a 100-billion-ecu-a-year global market by the year 2000 with the US industry revenues worth up to 52 billion dollars by that time and Japan's, 35 billion dollars. Telecommunications could be worth 6 per cent of GDP by early next century, instead of 1 to 2 per cent now; the worldwide telecommunications industry already accounts for a 285 billion ecu market for services and 82 billion ecu for equipment – and it is growing at 8 per cent a year alone for services. Environmental technology is another explosive growth sector. Europe is simply not up to speed, saddled as it is by too many monopolistic utilities and policies which are strangling innovation and growth.

Europe is also the odd man out of the technology triangle.

It buys far more high-tech products from the United States and Japan than it sells to them. In fact, it imports more technology from all its developed and rapidly developing partners than it exports. This gap is widening as Europe's high-tech sales overseas are growing at half the rate of its imports. And more of the link-ups between companies in this field are taking place between America and Japan, leaving Europe out in the cold.

Finding the cure

Even if world markets stood frozen in time, Europe's companies would still have to change. The complacent assumption that our industries can survive and thrive as they are would usher in stagnation and further decline. But there is a double imperative bearing upon the European economy: the shape, size and dynamics of world markets are themselves in a giddy state of flux.

First, those markets are getting bigger as world barriers fall. This has provoked a massive upsurge in overseas investment as companies seek to build a beachhead in markets far from home. According to the OECD, Foreign Direct Investment from OECD countries grew fourfold in the 1980s and much more rapidly than investments in the domestic economy, GDP or world trade. By 1990, the cumulative flow of OECD Foreign Direct Investment had reached 1.7 trillion dollars, or 8 per cent of world GDP. If Europe is to continue to lure a large slice of this investment, it must attract companies by improving roads, communications, tax incentives, access to European and outside markets as well as the skill and versatility of its workforce. Furthermore, if real interest rates or inflation are higher in Europe than in competing economies, this too will deflect investment away from the Union. If shareholders foresee a low return on their investment, they will obviously steer their companies and investments elsewhere.*

In addition, new players are entering the global economy as more nations from Asia, Latin America and Eastern Europe adopt open market policies. Europe has held on to its lead ever since the industrial revolution. It is uncomfortable to realize that perhaps for the first time in history, it needs now to think about catching up.

Europe needs to improve its performance in high technology. The continent is not rich in raw materials and gas, and has no overwhelming natural advantages. It does have a moderate climate conducive to farming, but as agriculture brings us just 3 per cent of our GDP, that will not solve Europe's economic woes. Our future prosperity will depend on our ability to take the technological lead by turning brainwaves into business ventures more successfully than at present. In terms of research, Europe still plants the best seedlings, but fails to propagate them into long-term industrial and commercial successes. Europe invented compact discs, yet hardly produces them any longer.

The 'Personal Digital Assistant Portable Computer', a pocket device which turns handwriting into digital script, was invented by European firms collaborating through 'Esprit', the Europe-wide research programme, yet they are now made and licensed in California. This catalogue of missed opportunity stems, among other factors, from the lack of risk capital to help firms through the developmental phase, inadequate links between universities and businesses and sometimes a lack of an adequate relationship between industry and defence research.

All this calls for a new attitude towards the very prospect

* According to the OECD, Europe's return on capital in the business sector has been consistently below those of Japan and the US throughout the 1970s, 80s and 90s. Worse still, this yield differential is now beginning to widen.

of change and innovation itself. Sclerosis has set in to attitudes as well as industry, and no amount of bright new policy will suffice if people do not adapt with it. The Asian miracle owes as much to the sheer energy with which its people approach their first-ever economic prosperity as to the sound economic policies of their governments. Instead of doing the bare minimum to stave off foreign competition, Europe needs to retake the initiative by improving its performance to the maximum. Europe needs to be the keen pupil at the front of the class rather than sitting in sullen silence at the back.

The limits on Europe's room for manoeuvre

The more interlinked economies become, the less Europe can reform its own economy with its hands totally untied. Europe cannot resort to home-made remedies if they interfere with its growing interdependence with the rest of the world. This interdependence is reaching world-shrinking proportions: many financial markets now operate twenty-four hours a day across the globe; any attempt to stabilize currencies by curbing speculation on European money markets would immediately send business to Wall Street, Tokyo and elsewhere. And the efficiency of a stockbroker is judged on his ability to pre-empt the dipping and rising of shares in seconds, not hours, days or weeks; European regulation must move at the speed of its best brokers rather than slowing down the markets themselves and driving business overseas.

Likewise, counterfeiters can steal the patent of a new product with the speed it takes to make a phone call or send a fax; the only way to protect copyright is to outrun the thief himself, getting the product to the customer fast, while arguing for stronger patent protection rules at international level.

A French bank no longer needs to process its customers' daily transactions on its own premises; it can hire a private company to do it more cheaply in Manila and send all the information back to Paris by satellite. Soon you may be able to make a phone call from Spain to Britain more cheaply via the United States by satellite than down the telephone lines of the British and Spanish national telecom companies. If Europe tries to regulate such practices out of the market, it will only drive more business to Kansas or Manila; far better to let European companies, public and private, take the American and Filipino competition head on.

It is also reasonable to expect that as China, Eastern Europe and the former Soviet Union come in from the cold of Communism, they will latch on to market forces with a verve that will oblige Western Europe to restructure its old traditional industries radically. Steel, textiles, non-ferrous metals and basic chemicals manufacturers will suffer whichever way Europe reacts to pressure from cut-price imports. Closing the shutters to imports will only put off the evil day, when instead we should make a virtue out of necessity by turning swiftly to higher value-added goods and services, winning new markets abroad while sustaining an open external trade policy at home. Expanding trade sharpens competition, stabilizes political relations, shores up democracy and ultimately tightens our security. This is discussed in greater detail in Chapter 6.

None the less, it is easy for Europeans to exaggerate the extent of their economic decay. After all, a factory closure makes a better story than a new production line, and people take to the street and attract the cameras when they lose jobs, not when they find them. The decline has struck hardest in manufacturing, while services have been booming. There are very few services you can see and touch, indeed many are still embryonic industries whose value has yet to catch the public eye; and yet services may hold the key to much of Europe's future prosperity: banking and insurance, legal services, accounting, medical and taxation services, telecommunications, real estate, postal services, the press, education, tourism, health and transport. Not only do these create wealth; they lubricate the rest of the European economy as well. In 1980, services brought in 42 per cent of Europe's earnings. This rose by 6 per cent to 48 per cent by 1990. Manufactured products fell from 26.5 per cent to 23.5 per cent over the same period. Despite the current buoyancy of the services sector, Europe is still not exploiting it for all it is worth. Segments of Europe's services sectors remain too shut off from full competitive forces, for example telecommunications, mortgage policies and life assurance.

Identifying the problems is the first prerequisite. Identifying the remedies is obviously vastly more difficult. But in terms of the European Union, the question that also needs to be asked is: *who* should be applying the remedies? Different authorities ranging from local councils and national governments up to the EU's Council of Ministers all pull different strings. That will never change, nor should it, for power needs exercising at the level most appropriate for the task in hand, however far down the ladder it may be. 'Subsidiarity' should apply here just as much as in any other area of decision-making. But even if action can often be taken at a national level, governments need to digest the fact that in many ways we are dealing with a single European economy.

Overcoming the folly of excessive state intervention

The beginning of wisdom is to recognize a blind alley when you see one.

Since the 1980s, recession-ridden Europe has been echoing to the sound of a new alarmist vocabulary: 'crisis' sectors cry out for special protection from market forces, while 'strategic' industries lobby for governments to bend the rules by offering money, going soft on debt repayment or turning a blind eye when companies gobble up their main rivals in a monopolistic fashion. Powerful companies argue a case for more government protection on the grounds that they hold the nation's future economic prosperity in their hands. In reality many know that without that protection they would fold.

Crisis sectors do definitely exist: Europe's once-great textiles, steel, shipbuilding and coal industries are battling to survive cut-throat competition from further afield. Whole communities are built around them, and the crisis is costing those communities dear in unemployment. Look, though, at past government attempts to help those sectors, for example in steel: 62 billion ecus worth of public money has gone to stave off crisis in the steel industry since 1975, with no lasting effect on the industry's ability to capture world markets. Similar stories abound in textiles, footwear, coal, shipbuilding, consumer electronics, parts of the car industry and most of agriculture and fisheries: a heady cocktail of subsidies, external trade barriers, ill-conceived mergers, some artificial pricing and in some cases 'strategic' research spending, has left segments of European industry hung over on the past, not equipped for the future. Europe has inadvertently created a dependency culture which slows productivity, stifles innovation, distorts and upsets the Single Market as well as draining the public purse.

Compare this to Europe's performance in sectors without massive state support. Of all the growth areas in the world economy, pharmaceuticals, chemicals, segments of the oil business, electrical engineering, electronics, telecommunications and food processing have so far proved the most lucrative. Europe is strong in pharmaceuticals, oil and food processing, as well as banking, insurance and some mechanical engineering, all areas where state influence has been relatively low. But in electronics and telecommunications, which are heavily subsidized, protected or regulated, Europe has slipped well behind the United States and Asia. Just seven of the world's thirty biggest, and six of the most profitable, electrical and electronics firms are European in origin. In consumer electronics, we are very weak. There is little left of the photocopier industry, and we are not well placed in the production of semi-conductors.

Yesterday, heavy industry employed very high numbers of workers, often paid below-average wages, and faced little competition from abroad. Today the tables have turned, leaving old industries to restructure at great cost while new ones can face the future without having to offload the baggage of the past. But that does not explain it all: Europe is still performing poorly in new sectors, where world growth is fastest; Europe is still losing market share in so-called 'capital goods' sectors – office machinery, data processing, processing plastics and telecom equipment.

A ten-point plan to revive Europe's ability to compete

As to the World Economic Forum's eight key ingredients cited earlier – domestic economic strength, internationalization, government, finance, infrastructure, management, science and technology, and people – the European Union and its member countries have a shared role in blending them together to produce a more competitive industry. For example, governments are largely responsible for creating a sound economic base, but *de facto* they are bound to collaborate closely over the use of interest rates, exchange rates and other tools to achieve it. And on 'internationalization', they chose to present a common face to the outside world as far back as 1957 through the EU's common trade policy (based on Article 113 of the Treaty of Rome), jointly deciding how high to set the bar to imports and when and how to lower it. Joint European laws are now making banking, insurance and stockbroking a Europe-wide business, and customers will soon find it easier to send money across borders as a result of work done at EU level.

There is, therefore, considerable symbiosis between separate and joint actions taken by European governments to restore competitiveness. The EU and governments together now need to implement measures to reform the European economy with actions at national, regional and local level. For convenience I set out the kind of policies that are needed as a ten-point plan although some of them are discussed in greater detail elsewhere in this book. Not all ten points are new, nor will they all have equal impact. But they are timely and complementary, and if applied consistently by all EU governments irrespective of ideological hue, will create a stronger, more solid but flexible economic backbone on which European industry can seek out and exploit future markets with a more skilled workforce than ever before.

I: FULL IMPLEMENTATION OF THE EUROPEAN SINGLE MARKET

The European Single Market needs to be completed and the benefits fully reaped before we can say the job is signed, sealed and delivered, and before it is worthy of the name. The aim is to remove barriers to the flow of goods, money, services and people across the EU's internal borders. The vast majority have already gone, but statistics can be deceptive and some major hurdles remain. Although 95 per cent of the Community's original 282 proposed laws were achieved by the end 1992 deadline, EU nations still do not see eye-to-eye on some veterinary controls, rules for dual use goods, certain aspects of intellectual property protection such as legal protection of database designs and industrial models, indirect taxation, and the recognition of all each other's vocational qualifications; and despite herculean efforts by Brussels, they have still failed to agree a single instrument enabling businesses to offset profits in one country against losses in another by incorporating as 'European' companies.

After creation comes implementation. The signing of a market-building measure by European ministers is just the beginning of a long and arduous process of scrutiny by national parliaments before it becomes law throughout the European Union.

After implementation, and indeed before it too, comes enforcement. The European Commission must police the Single Market rigorously, cajoling governments to transpose rules already agreed by their ministers. It must also weed out new barriers that have crept in on spurious 'technical' grounds as industries seek to fend off competition from elsewhere in Europe. Recalcitrant governments should, if necessary, be taken more regularly to the European Court of Justice, newly reinforced for this and other tasks under the Maastricht Treaty.

As and when the market gathers new legislation to smooth out fresh areas of business, the EU should take earlier and more careful note of the views of industry, consumers and other interest groups. More extensive use of consultative Green Papers would produce more precise rules, help strip the EU machine of unwarranted secrecy and reduce the number of legislative mistakes that damage business by adding unnecessary costs. It would also enhance the Union's own image. On new legislation, the Union should assess the costs and benefits more systematically, while perpetually scouring existing rules for provisions that become redundant and burdensome as business practices change. The Union should cut out the fat from its Single Market rules while reinforcing those that are indispensable for stimulating cross-border business.

2: A STRICTER POLICY ON STATE SUBSIDIES

If the Single Market is the playing field, then Europe's common policy against anti-competitive behaviour is the referee. Some of the biggest fouls are currently committed by governments themselves, which still inject about 2 per cent of GDP, 4.3 per cent of public spending and 3.5 per cent of gross value added of their economies into their favourite industries. Persistent whistle-blowing by the European Commission over the last decade has borne fruit: state subsidies to manufacturers have dropped from 40.6 billion ecu in 1986 to 34 billion ecu in 1990 (based on 1989 prices). Admittedly, they are now applied less through favouritism to national 'champion' companies than through concern for backward regions, but there is still a long way to go. The biggest spenders are the authorities in Germany, France and Italy, but when measured against the number of employees, Greece, Spain and Italy pay out the most. Forty-two per cent of these state subsidies are aimed at general objectives rather than specific companies, such as improving research and innovation, building up small and medium companies and boosting exports; 38 per cent goes to help lagging regions catch up with their richer neighbours, while 20 per cent is channelled into specific sectors of industry, notably shipbuilding, coal, steel and others where markets and jobs are shrinking.

Europe still needs to continue pruning state subsidies harshly, but not to remove them altogether; for it is not so much the size as the ill-use of government aid that damages industry's ability to compete. Governments have tended to give in to those that shout loudest, usually large companies in crisis-ridden sectors, thus enabling them to put off the inevitable, painful streamlining they need in order to secure their future. Under strong pressure from Brussels, the folly of such spending has begun to dawn on cash-strapped governments, which now channel a greater portion of their aid than ever before to help their poorer regions to catch up economically. Europe must continue to cut subsidies across the board while redirecting them into areas which need aid most and which will use aid best: if governments were to reduce their overall subsidies by 20 per cent each year, this could unleash around 20 billion ecu in four years, giving their treasuries some vital headroom to improve training and upgrade Europe's technology policy, for example. Subsidies should equip industry for the future, not lash it to the past.

The Commission only has the power to challenge individual subsidies that are in breach of the rules; it cannot impose an overall target for the reduction of subsidies. Such a target could only be agreed by the member states themselves, and it is high time that such a target was agreed.

In crisis industries, governments should judge a company's demand for help against its proven commitment to slim down production, and if necessary its workforce, to the point that it will not need more aid in future. When considering subsidies, governments must ask themselves whether they will provide the best long-term chance of generating sustainable wealth and employment for the region, town or village in question. And when funding poorer regions, governments should aim to enrich the topsoil of the economy so that when companies come to invest, they put down roots and stay because the conditions for growth are good. This means building better transport and communications, training a more skilled workforce and providing start-up capital for small companies on which the bigger ones will come to rely. And it means curbing aid to regions which waste it, or simply cannot spend it.

3: A SINGLE EUROPEAN CURRENCY
The drive to complete the European Single Market itself has only been possible in a period of exchange rate stability.

Recession, deepened by the strains of German reunification, has tugged relentlessly at the bands of Europe's Exchange Rate Mechanism, finally stretching them so far apart that the Single Market itself is under threat. It would be wrong to overlook the economic gains made during Europe's decade of currency stability under the Exchange Rate Mechanism. It would be equally wrong to force Europe's economies back into an ever-tighter straitjacket when they clearly need to breathe deeply and recover by lowering interest rates in their own time and stimulating growth. But in the longer run the case for a single currency to improve competitiveness is stronger than ever. This is an important point in a recovery programme for European industry, and is discussed in more detail in Chapter 4.

4: ENCOURAGING THE GROWTH OF SMALL AND MEDIUM COMPANIES

While it would still be unfair to say that multinationals prefer robots to people, they are no longer the mass employers they once were. New technology and robotics have led to a striking decline in the number of blue-collar workers manning the production lines. This trend is unlikely to be reversed. And governments are less well placed than ever to step in and bear the cost of job creation, for they are tightening their budgetary belts enough as it is, and will have to tighten them further as Europe's population ages. That leaves small and medium-sized enterprises. SMEs (those with under 500 employees) already provide over two-thirds of the European Union's employment, and they created an estimated three-quarters of all new jobs in the Union over the last three years as well as producing some two-thirds of value added in most European countries. As well as being ideal job-creators, SMEs also fill the cracks in Europe's competitiveness, streamlining bigger firms either by working *for* them more cheaply, or *against* them, forcing them to cut costs themselves. Encouraging SMEs must become a central pillar of Europe's drive to improve its economic performance.

Several policy threads already exist, and governments must pull them closer together at European and national level. First, Europe must remove the burdens on small business, slimming down the paperwork required of SMEs, integrating SMEs more closely into the Single Market and fine-tuning the EU's existing rules to curb late payment that can cripple them with cash-flow problems.

Secondly, the EU must coax them further into the economic mainstream. They may be an indispensable element in that mainstream, but they do not always have a powerful voice, as the area of public procurement illustrates: SMEs are often jostled out of lucrative government contracts or excluded from publicly funded research programmes because of an excessive focus on bigger firms with louder voices, or through the insuperable burden of expensive form-filling. If SMEs are to ride out the recession and fulfil their pivotal role in the economy, they need to be drawn into the mainstream of all future economic policy. Offering extensive possibilities for SMEs to create networks among themselves is one route worth comprehensive examination. This means broking SMEs into joint research projects across borders, while using EU rules, notably in competition and government procurement, to stop them suffocating under the monopoly power of their larger rivals. Above all, governments and the Union itself should assess even more carefully the impact of every new rule on small business before putting rules forward. The European Commission currently does this, but not with anywhere near the vigour that it deserves.

5: BOOSTING THE PRODUCTIVITY OF PUBLIC SPENDING

Most treasuries guard the public purse so jealously that they would only see it shift to Brussels over their dead bodies. It rightly remains the sovereign preserve of governments to spend the money of the taxpayers who have elected them. None the less, the Union itself has a sizeable budget for which it is answerable to the European taxpayer. At the Edinburgh Summit in December 1992, government leaders agreed the EC's seven-year spending guidelines up until the end of 1999, and they are unlikely to approve more funds for Europe before then. The Union must, therefore, spend well. It must allocate staff better, shifting officials faster to fill new posts created as Europe defines new areas for joint policy action. And it must curb fraud, which although wildly exaggerated by an often ill-wishing press, nevertheless topped 500 million ecu in the 1991–2 spending year according to the EU's Inspector-General. This of course only represents identified fraud.

In any organization, the Commission included, there is dead wood and the odd rotten apple among an overwhelmingly loyal and efficient staff. And there are administrative loopholes through which fraud can escape unnoticed, particularly in high-spending sectors like agriculture where excessively complex, overlapping rules sometimes inadvertently open opportunities for the calculating professional fraudster. This requires far tighter control in the Commission when allocating funds and dispensing contracts, with proper quality control to ensure the money yields the intended results and that it is indeed spent at all. When new rules are needed they should be drafted so as to ensure that they are simple, comprehensible and unambiguous. The fight against fraud is also perpetually hampered by mutual finger-pointing between the Brussels Commission, national governments and customs authorities. Less recrimination and more cooperation is the only means of stopping some EU funding from being spirited away or simply wasted. More ex-post analysis and scrutiny of spending programmes by independent experts to judge whether the EU's expenditure did indeed fulfil its objective is also required.

Another dimension to fraud of increasing concern is that concerning textile imports into the European Union. In order to get around the textile quotas some fraudulent exporters to the EU market declare a false origin, thereby ensuring greater market access. The extent of this fraud is worrying, but should decrease as the multifibre agreement is phased out. Until then, the EU should cooperate with the US and other like-minded countries to ensure that the agreed rules and quotas are fully obeyed by textile exporters to Europe.

6: CHANNELLING PRIVATE CAPITAL TO DEVELOP TRANS-EUROPEAN NETWORKS

Europe's infrastructure can sometimes seem like a patchwork of exquisitely embroidered fabrics hastily sewn together into a rather tatty-looking quilt. If we expect European industry to behave as one economy in one market, then we need to plan our roads, railways, ports, airways, information networks, telephones, pipelines and electricity grids as one integrated whole. The European Union has already agreed to loosen up access to major financing for a series of so-called 'Trans-European Networks',* completing Europe's existing infrastructure so that it spans the entire Single Market.

These initiatives are of vital importance to boost Europe's flagging competitiveness, and should be accelerated and strengthened, with a view to completing a major part of the external networks by the end of the century. The European Commission's White Paper on Growth, Competitiveness and Employment estimates that some 250 billion ecu are needed

---

* Under Article 129 of the Treaty, the Community is asked to promote the inter-connection and inter-operability of the Community's different regions, including linking islands, landlocked areas and the peripheral regions. The great advantage of these projects is that they open up new economic potential, they create jobs and they will reduce the costs of doing business.

to bring transport and energy links up to standard by the end of the century. A further 150 billion ecu would be needed to modernize information links with cable and satellite-based radio communication, digital networks, electronic mail and images, as well as to promote training, medicine and other services by telephone link. The European Union must play a pivotal role by helping countries gain access to private capital. Such infrastructure networks clearly cannot simply be paid for out of the public purse. The effective harnessing of private finance is the key. Only by giving private finance a return on its capital through tolls or other such devices and reducing some of the financial or administrative risks involved is this going to be reasonably feasible.

Money aside, the Union must successfully harmonize 'technical standards' to reduce the cost of connecting networks from one country to another. Put simply, this means ensuring that Belgian trains fit German tracks, that British electricity can travel across French grids and vice versa, and that Spain, Italy and Greece all use compatible digital equipment as they extend telephone lines throughout their territory. Failure will cost us dear: for example, the new high-speed TGV train between Paris, Brussels, Cologne and Amsterdam could cost each city over 50 per cent extra to operate if they work to different technical standards.

The planning of the trans-European networks at EU level should remain skeletal, leaving contractors to justify the details to private investors rather than conforming to a masterplan based more on geographical symmetry and political pressure than on sound economic realities.

7: IMPROVING THE VERSATILITY OF EUROPE'S WORKFORCE
Ridding Europe's labour market of the rigidities that stunt economic growth and swell unemployment will require a more creative response than perhaps all the other remedies to

be applied to Europe's economic ills. *Creative* because much of Europe's chequered history of industrial exploitation and antagonistic labour relations has left some workforces deeply sceptical of reform and anxious to use their powers to halt such reform. Such is the distrust within industry that many workers presume 'flexibility' simply means derisory wages, hiring and firing and a callous disregard for health and safety in the workplace. And *creative* because national governments are sceptical of perceived interference from the European Union at all if it only involves an attempt to bring about a consensus view of the right policy to apply, without any attempt to impose it by legislation.

Brussels' main role must be to remove barriers to workers seeking jobs, or students and teachers studying, abroad; to ensure their qualifications, if adequate, are recognized universally; and to act as a clearing-house for the best training and retraining schemes on offer throughout Europe. There is a serious mismatch between the skills people learn and those they require for the posts available. The Union cannot solve this alone, but it can contribute to the flow of information guiding firms to the most suitable vocational training schemes. When workers lose their jobs, Brussels should leave the handling to governments themselves; it is in finding them new ones and kitting them out with the right training that governments should seek to act together through the EU. This is explored in greater detail in Chapter 5. Nevertheless the European Union has a role in creating a market for training, encouraging cross-frontier development projects and fostering links between European universities and training establishments. These policies will help improve the versatility of Europe's labour market.

8: IMPROVING EUROPE'S RESEARCH AND DEVELOPMENT

It is tempting to view European research as a steady stream of good ideas being robbed by our less inventive but more businesslike Japanese and American competitors. Righteous indignation at the plagiarism of our partners will do little to solve our research problems, as well as being thin on evidence. It is far better to analyse where Europe is going wrong and put it right. Europe spends just 2 per cent of GDP on research, while Japan spends half that amount again and the US spends around 2.6 per cent. Europe also has proportionately fewer researchers and engineers. European research is indeed stronger at conceiving ideas at the embryonic, pre-competitive stage than at exploiting them in the market place, where tangible profits show. At European rather than national level, research funding has tended to produce fine technological ideas with many potential commercial spin-offs, without tuning in to consumer demand and channelling them into a set of industrial priorities for the future. Take 'green' motoring, for example: drivers are addicted to the personal freedom a car provides, but they are bothered by the fumes; this creates the perfect recipe for the environment-friendly car. Europe produces good basic environmental research as well as top-quality cars, but its contribution to 'green' motoring amounts to little more than the belated introduction of lead-free fuel and catalytic converters. Are we waiting, once again, for Japan and the US to get there first and develop the green car, thereby setting the world-wide standards which we will have to follow?

This may well be a problem of planning as much as funding. After all, the Clinton Administration is seeking to open up a vast new information network linking databases right across the country in order to tap lucrative new markets. The project involves speeding up the introduction of new high-speed networks, computer systems and communication technologies and applying them to new areas of the economy. Similarly, Japan plans its research and development decades ahead of Europe. Surely Europe must get to grips quickly with the same information revolution that is upon us all, whether this is done in relation to EU-funded research, national research or even private-sector research? Those economies that implement these sophisticated information networks first will have a considerable comparative economic advantage. Europe has to move fast.

First, we need to ensure ideas are picked up more readily from initial conception right through to the final product, setting firm competitive priorities to prevent good ideas from falling by the wayside. Secondly, we need closer collaboration between European countries, enabling researchers and inventors to spread the net Europe-wide in search of the ideal partner, and putting an end to pointless competition between EU countries themselves. Thirdly, research aid should be tailored more precisely to those who need it most, often small and medium companies. Fourthly, Europe needs proper quality control on its joint research programmes, enabling it swiftly to abandon programmes which look unlikely to yield industrial profits. Fifthly: opening up Europe's protected markets will stimulate economic research in new areas (see below). This way European research would readily justify its final need: more money.

9: DEREGULATING AND PRIVATIZING EUROPE'S REMAINING SEGMENTED MARKETS

Europe is undergoing a sea-change in its approach to the deregulation and privatization of its state-controlled industries. In the 1980s European governments viewed deregulation and privatization suspiciously as an American craze sweeping evangelically across Britain. As it privatized one bastion of British state industry after another, the British government was seen as selling the family silver in pursuit of an ideology which improved services for the privileged few while neglecting those most in need. As such, deregulation was to be kept firmly at bay on the other side of the Channel. And yet it is now catching on right across Europe. France, where the state has been the pivot of the economy since Louis XIV, is embarking on a major privatization programme as it realizes that some of its state industries may actually survive rather well on their own; even Italy is seeking to dissolve its massive and inefficient state holding companies, partly in the hope that the country's crippling corruption will dissipate with it. And the sheer gusto with which Eastern Europe has latched on to privatization is steeling their nerves. A mixture of competition, corruption, budgetary belt-tightening, and a certain pleasant surprise at the British experience, are prompting governments to hand the reins of industry over to industry itself.

Deregulation is as important as privatization and it is here that the European Union must maintain a specific role in pushing the process along. To privatize or not is a question for the member states to decide. In the case of deregulation, however, the Commission has the right to act. Through the use of EU transport and competition rules, it has sought to stop Europe's big airlines grounding their smaller rivals and keeping airfares high as a result; and it is gradually increasing an airline's right to carry passengers between any two European cities and in ever larger numbers, creating an 'open skies' regime which, if state subsidies are curbed successfully, will force the excessive number of existing major European carriers to shrink. And the EU is consulting industry before launching final plans to deregulate parcel services, while fostering greater competition in telephone calls. These policies must be pursued with vigour.

Several key sectors remain firmly in the hands of the state, largely because governments are flinching in the face of fierce trade union opposition and public fears that vital services will be eroded in outlying areas. These fears, while understandable, are exaggerated. Deregulation need not lead to fewer basic services being provided in the less accessible corners of Europe, and in pressing for deregulation the Commission has accepted a social obligation to give every citizen a decent mail, telephone and power service wherever he may live.

Europe must revive its flagging plans to deregulate the oil, gas and electricity markets so that its airlines, factories, and other major energy users can buy from the cheapest, most efficient suppliers in Europe. This means removing legal barriers – removing the right of one national supplier to monopolize its entire national market, and technical barriers – allowing any power station to use the pylons, pipelines and other parts of the energy 'grid' in any other European country. These barriers have no part to play in a unified Single Market, and I see no reason why the Commission should hesitate to apply the competition policy powers which are entrusted to it to bring these barriers down.

The European Union must focus not just on energy, post, telecommunications and airlines, but also on railways. Here too there will come a point as with other state monopolies where the choice will be between deregulation and full privatization. Forbidden from insisting on privatization itself, the Commission is none the less obliged (under the Treaty of Rome) to ensure that Europe's governments do not distort competition by the unfair granting of privileges to state-run or state-sponsored monopolistic utilities. These special privileges can hinder the private sector's ability to compete with their government-owned rivals by selling cheaper gas or electricity across borders, running international rail freight services or sending parcels abroad, and the Single Market undoubtedly suffers as a result. Europe's market will never be truly single until the monopoly grip of the big utilities is loosened both domestically and internationally. And not attacking this problem means stunting innovation and the creative pursuit of new value-added goods and services right across the European market.

10: STRENGTHENING EUROPE'S TRADE REGIME BOTH INSIDE AND OUTSIDE ITS BORDERS

As explained more fully in Chapter 6, trade is the oxygen that fills the lungs of the European economy. It is one of the oldest of the Union's 'common policies', so European governments should have learned by now to speak in unison to the outside world. The more we come to depend on foreign trade and the international rules that police it, the less our domestic protection will be needed. None the less, we must keep up our defences against unfair trade practice, sharpening them and using them more efficiently and accurately, but only when solid evidence dictates such action, not when governments bend to industrial pressure from within Europe. Recent proposals adopted by European ministers will ensure that Europe's trade defence instruments are now much more efficient than in the past, and will help restore confidence among European industry. These are discussed in Chapter 6.

Trade is doubly important to Europe, which is more dependent on imports and exports than even the United States or Japan. Our future prosperity thus lies in our ability to find new markets overseas. The European Union needs to develop a more coherent policy through which we can forcefully encourage our partners to open their markets as wide as we open ours. But we must not resort to the use of offensive legal weapons to prise open foreign markets where there has been no breach of trade rules, as have some of the world's major trading nations, for this merely undermines the GATT, where the biggest market-opening of all takes place multilaterally.

What we do have to do, however, is to encourage European industry to exploit the opportunities open to it in the fast-growing new markets of Asia and Latin America. In the future we will also need to work more closely with other like-minded countries to open markets that are unfairly closed to our exporters.

Conclusion

Fixing a price-tag on Europe's loss of competitiveness is a highly imprecise exercise. Indeed, many of the causes are well-nigh impossible to calculate; how do you measure business confidence in francs, dollars or ecu? And yet even if you allow for a massive margin of inaccuracy, the potential gains of specific measures are so colossal that they defy even the most nit-picking statistician. A single currency could yield over 19 billion ecu; phased reductions in state subsidies might yield over 20 billion ecu; tighter use of the EU budget and further clamp-down on fraud could perhaps yield several billion ecu; cutting world tariffs by an average of 30 per cent or more under the Uruguay Round will boost total world income by over 1 per cent, generating extra global business worth around 270 billion dollars, according to the OECD and GATT Secretariats.

Making these savings will be of substantial benefit to the European economy. They will lighten the burden on industries and on governments; but they will not restore competitiveness on their own. The roots of Europe's industrial crisis go far deeper, running right back down to the core of Europe's very economic success: the industrial revolution. European development drove the world economy for so long that it was only as late as the Second World War that it dawned on Europe that industrial leadership was no longer a birthright. Over forty years later, that humbling fact is still sinking in. It left Europe with a disabling tendency to put off the evil day, or to assume, like Charles Dickens' Mr

Micawber, that 'something will turn up' to pull European industry back from the brink. The trouble is, it often has, but in the form of government protection, rules and regulations that stifle creativity, innovation and business enterprise.

The 1980s appeared to change all that, as a fresh wave of prosperity in Europe brought renewed thirst for a Single Market, a single currency, a single infrastructure network and other vehicles of long-term stability and growth. It also ushered in a new readiness on the part of governments, either independently or through the European Union itself, to take a bolder view of open trade: egged on by the European Commission, governments began cutting subsidies, withdrawing partially from the control of industry, and forging a trade policy that made Europe look less like a fortress and more like an open though well-fenced paddock. Recession has undoubtedly shaken their will, but not permanently.

Europe's business and political leaders are now fully seized of the need to catch up with our economic competitors, doubly so as more come on stream in Asia, Eastern Europe and Latin America. They are searching fervently for cures to Europe's industrial ills. This search will bear fruit if they encourage companies to exploit the full breadth of European potential for all it is worth, notably in research and technology. But the search for competitiveness carries a risk: Europe could look so hard into the distance that it fails to notice what is lying at its feet; its greatest chance of turning industry around is to sustain the Single Market and build the macro-economic, research, trade, labour and infrastructure policies that will help, but also oblige, industry to make that market work, and to thrust its new-found competitiveness outwards.

CHAPTER 5

Looking After Europe

There are two common caricatures of the European Union, both of which have earned it unjust criticism. For some, it is an aloof, would-be avuncular figure, fixing lofty rules to make life easier for big business, assuming the benefits will some day trickle down to the man in the street, but rarely stooping low enough to see whether that actually happens. For others, it is a meddlesome housemaid, taking on new chores to keep herself busy, wielding her duster through the cobwebs and annoying the mistress of the house as she breaks the family china. As always, the true nature of the Union falls somewhere in between the caricatures; but exaggerated though they are, they do illustrate two extremes which Europe should seek carefully to avoid.

Rather than assuming the role of distant uncle or bothersome nanny, the Union should act more as the steward of Europe, looking after its people and its natural resources without over-regulating the pattern of their lives. Stewardship flows from the idea of Europe as a Union of peoples, not just a common market in which to sell their wares. It means bringing European agriculture closer to the market place while recognizing the concerns of people who have tilled the soil for centuries; it means narrowing the gap between the rich and poor regions of Europe while making both richer, not poorer; it means establishing the right of men and women to earn equal pay, something for which national laws hardly existed when the Community was founded. Stewardship also means matching Europe's need for industrial growth with its need to protect its fragile environment, and ensuring that equality of opportunity flourishes between the sexes, the races, the regions and the nations themselves.

Can this concept of stewardship be reconciled with the principle of subsidiarity? I believe it can. For subsidiarity means not doing what the individual member states can do best on their own; but also taking action where only European action can achieve agreed objectives. The concept of a community, as opposed to a simple free-trade area, has been accepted for a generation. It necessarily involves the idea that the security, prosperity and harmony of those who belong to it can only be achieved if the peoples of Europe come closer together where excessive polarization would endanger that very security, prosperity and harmony. How far one need go in that process of coming together will always be a matter of judgement and even of controversy, but whatever the agreed degree of coming together, it is the Union that has to act as the steward of that process.

If Europe is to perform that stewardship responsibly, it must always search for the consensus that exists, and seek to shape it where much-needed agreement eludes us. It involves striking a delicate balance between intervention and abstention, and taking great care not to clash with subsidiarity. For example, countries may differ radically over how interventionist they think the Union should be, but they still agree on the need to foster and protect Europe's limited natural and human resources. Europe must find the consensus on how to exploit, but not exhaust, those resources, maximizing the ability of our industry to compete without ruining our environment or the social fabric on which our industry is based.

On social policy, finding that consensus will be an uphill struggle, for when it comes to the rights of workers, the unemployed, pregnant mothers, adolescents and the elderly,

Europe's diversity is at its greatest. Creating a free market for goods is easy compared to deciding how workers should influence corporate decision-making, for instance.

At the most basic level, a 'European social consensus' of sorts does exist. No EU country allows its citizens to descend into penury and distress before the government intervenes. A basic safety net exists throughout the Union, written in constitutions or set by tradition, even if the net is strung higher above the breadline in some countries than in others. Democracy, too, is a key ingredient in that consensus, for in all EU states the representatives of the different sides of the economy are encouraged to reach agreement in order to avoid the need for governments themselves to intervene.

Though they all share the same roots, quite different models have developed in different countries, making the social consensus even harder, though by no means impossible, to discern. France and Germany both allow workers a major say in company decision-making, though in different ways and at different levels. The *Conseils d'Entreprise* in France are less pervasive than the German system of *Mitbestimmung*, or worker co-management, under which employee representatives actually take part in company board meetings. Germany also allows for the fixing of broad wage targets in advance every year at regional or national level, contrasting strongly with Britain's belief that managers and trade unions should be left to settle such matters between themselves without government-led concertation. Most European nations settle for models in between: eleven out of the twelve countries have or are actively seeking a 'social pact' agreement with their trade unions. The contents vary, but they all include understandings about pay.

Some argue that Europe has one specifically 'European' model of society, as distinct from that of the United States or the former Communist countries, and that one set of social standards should flow from that. This view is fraught with contradictions and outright inaccuracies; if such a model ever existed, which I doubt, it is changing beyond recognition. And that change is driven above all by the fact that the kind of welfare net a nation can afford depends more than ever before on a nation's overall wealth, not on the ambition or 'generosity' of its politicians.

The role of the state already differs radically from one country to another. That role is evolving once again: Italy, for example, whose real and potential wealth lies with its flourishing private companies, is shedding the old skin of excessive state intervention, in the hope of improving efficiency and ridding industry of the corruption that has crippled the competitiveness of the public sector. An even more drastic experiment in privatization has been occurring in the former East Germany, where the Treuhandanstalt is selling off the region's Communist industrial inheritance at great speed. Whether buffeted by reunification in Germany or grinding inefficiency in Italy, European industry and society are in transition. Industry *may* be moving closer to the market place, and governments *may* be approaching a common desire not to live beyond their means any longer but all talk of a single industrial or social 'model' would be as inaccurate now as it was in the past.

Rather than legislating for a consensus that does not yet exist, governments must ask themselves whether they can afford the kind of social legislation they want; and the European Union itself must ask whether differing national rules jeopardize the smooth running of the Single Market and hinder economic expansion. Only where cross-border problems do occur should the Union legislate, otherwise subsidiarity requires that it should refrain. In this way there will be a European social policy which creates and sustains jobs rather than suffocating them, allowing for diversity of nations while rooting out anything which genuinely threatens trade between them.

The Union's founding Treaty of Rome produced few social laws with any real teeth, but the Single European Act, signed in 1985, quickened the pace somewhat. European governments agreed that the differing costs implied by different levels of health and safety standards between countries risked upsetting the balance of competition within Europe's internal market. So they agreed to forfeit their right to veto measures which sought to improve the health and safety of people while at work, on the basis that these were 'internal market' measures and nothing more. An extremely generous interpretation of this concept has subsequently led to new laws on maternity leave and maternity pay, and even to a flirtation with banning work on Sundays. It was a short step to the adoption of the Social Charter, in which all Union countries except Britain solemnly declared that they had 'agreed on the need to promote living and working conditions for workers so as to make possible their harmonization'. This in turn gave birth to an 'Action Programme' of concrete measures. Some of these are positive, genuinely improving the welfare of the workforce without interrupting the flow of business; others go one dangerous step further, threatening to impinge on a company's ability to stay competitive.

On the positive side, the action programme produced a framework for improving the health and safety of workers, embracing specific rules on exposure to noxious chemical, physical and biological substances, and standards of protection for those working in factories or on trains, fishing boats and other forms of transport. On the negative side, it spawned new proposals governing working hours, part-time work, the employment of children and adolescents, the treatment of pregnant women, and the way workers are informed and consulted on corporate decisions taken by their board of directors.

The United States has taken a similar leap towards centralizing its control over social laws. The federal government can decide job protection rules over the heads of America's state authorities, based on the legal fiction that a job created in Michigan could be a job lost in Minnesota. Some would argue that employment is a crucial part of Europe's Single Market, so why should Europe not follow America's example and regulate it?

This argument is based on false logic and should not go unchallenged. Some see minimum working hours in terms of humanitarian values, indispensable to the fabric of all 'civilized' communities, while others point out that the European Single Market could not function without them, and fair competition would begin to fray at the edges without common rules on employment. And yet if pressed, proponents of this line would concede that the reality is that some governments simply find the Single Market politically unpalatable without a social 'dimension', and they need measures to sugar the pill for Europe's trade unions as they face the chill winds of cross-border competition. This is a purely political argument which most governments accept, happy to adopt social laws as worthy targets for a socially responsible Union, but safe in the knowledge that those laws will not bite for a long time, if at all, both because of the sheer pressure of Europe's diversity and because of the effect on European competitiveness and employment of persisting with them.

I am not calling for a repeal of all existing Union social rules, but rather for far more rigorous analysis of their costs and benefits, and of Europe's need to fix them collectively. Like all other rules, they should be subjected to the subsidiarity test, filtered out if found to be superfluous or excessive, but kept and enforced properly if deemed indispensable to Europe's cross-border business. After all, there is abundant evidence of successful national and regional rules: local legislation exists right across the Union on early-closing days for shops; the UK's Equal Opportunities Commission is far more effective than practically anything elsewhere in Europe; and there are rules which ensure that local working traditions continue: young Danes, for example, are specifically authorized to begin work at five o'clock in the morning during the strawberry-picking season, and provision exists for young Britons to rise with the lark and deliver newspapers, or for young Germans to be employed on farms. All this is done under proper supervision, and with proper regard for the health and welfare of the youngsters concerned.

Can it really be said that these national variants impede fair competition in the Union or damage Europe's sense of community? To suggest that this is so is simply politically correct nonsense – and it is becoming even less politically correct as each month goes by. To judge the best level at which social rules should be defined, consensus is the key, and we should start with the existing consensus, only seeking to create a different one if the reasons for doing so are very powerful indeed. It is up to local authorities, for example, to decide for or against early-closing days, according to whether it suits local shopkeepers and their clientele, most of whom will live and shop locally. And why not? Rules governing the sacking of workers need determining nationally, however, for the dividing line between fair and unfair dismissal is reflected in the views of a society as a whole. Likewise, EU states should only legislate at the collective European level where there is enough of a common inheritance to muster a genuine European consensus. They share a common distaste for poverty, and a common market – that much is certain; they are developing a common desire to sharpen the competitive edge of their industries – that is emerging too; and most of them support industrial democracy, although not, as yet, in identical ways; but they emphatically do *not* see eye-to-eye on shift work, part-time employment and maternity leave, whatever they may have promised on paper in order to move with the flow.

The absence of such a consensus can lead to play-acting by member states anxious to prove their social credentials, with some amusing results. In 1992 a Commission proposal called for 'minimum safety and health requirements for transport activities and workplaces on means of transport'. The section on Floors, Walls and Ceilings contained the clause: 'The floors or workplaces must be of non-slip material unless this is incompatible with the purpose of the floor in question.' Who other than indoor ski specialists is going to design floors for people to slip on? When I queried the clause, I was told airily that 'this is all the Ministers will accept, so we have to write it like this; we cannot put any *real* standards in'.

This may appear harmless, knockabout stuff; but there are more disturbing motives shifting behind the veils of Europe's apparent social consensus, begging one serious question: do Europe's wealthier nations always have the best interests of their poorer neighbours at heart when pushing for a high level of social protection across the Union? During the run-up to the signing in 1989 of the Social Charter, there was substantial anecdotal evidence of fears in Northern Europe that the Union's Southern half would undercut prices and poach jobs from the North by exploiting their poorer social standards. And yet if Portugal, Greece, Southern Italy and parts of Spain, not to mention Ireland and much of Britain, are to revive their economies, they must be allowed to exploit what for some may be their only comparative advantage: lower costs and cheaper labour.

That comparative advantage may flow from social, historical or even natural distinctions between Europe's nations, and the Union must respect those differences. The climate, for example, which brings Italian children outdoors all summer while leaving British children to watch the August drizzle from indoors, also affects the economy: avocados grow well in Spain, strawberries in Denmark and flowers in Holland, but wage costs differ radically in all three countries. Should they be harmonized? In Spain, family bonds are strong and relatives tend to live close by, so young working mothers might not rely so heavily on maternity leave. Is this not part of a nation's comparative advantage too? But one blanket set of restrictive social norms for the whole Union could make this task harder. Ministers have frequently told me behind closed doors that to enforce some of the rules they feel politically obliged to accept would burden their industries with costs way beyond their level of productivity.

In an ideal market, business will gravitate to the place where it is performed best and at the lowest cost. In 1959, that was exactly the platform on which the Community was built, with France supplying the food and Germany the machines, although the balance has, of course, now evened out. European nations must retain the right to undercut their neighbours and keep the continent competitive in the process. The European Union's 'structural funds' for supporting backward or declining regions are crucial, but no transfer of funds to the poorer parts of Europe could sweeten the loss of their comparative advantage; Germany, after all, is rich because it sells good products well. Greece may one day be able to say the same, if encouraged to sell what it makes best at good prices. But efforts to close the gap forcibly, obliging Greece, for example, to carry social costs its economy cannot bear, will not hoist Greece up to German levels of prosperity; rather they will drag Greece down, gradually pulling the whole of Europe down with it.

If we overburden our companies at home, they will fail when fighting for world markets, the lifeline to Europe's continuing prosperity. We need, therefore, to look hard at anything which adds to that burden. The European Commission systematically assesses the impact of new EU laws on the industry they cover before launching them. This 'impact assessment' system, which judges whether measures boost jobs, increase paperwork or raise costs to the employer, needs improving: the use of the assessment currently sometimes takes more account of he who drafts the law than he whose business will be affected, so the Commission should actively seek views from industry itself as part of the assessment process. It also needs widening and deepening in scope: widening to gauge the full impact on the whole of European industry's ability to compete, and deepening to assess the comparative impact of alternatives, including inaction. Europe has been outperformed by Japan and the United States for many years, but the Commission has never seriously compared its taxation, employment, environment or other proposals, and their costs, with those existing in Japan or the United States, before bringing them forward.

There is now an even more pressing need to consider cost: the pressure on Europe's overburdened social security systems is growing intolerable, and they will not withstand it for ever. The proportion of pensioners is rising as people live longer, and pension costs are spinning out of control, particularly in countries with pay-as-you-earn systems. The strain is showing on national budgets: for several years now, France has been siphoning funds from its general tax revenue to help pay its pensioners, even though French taxation and national insurance are in theory strictly segregated. Life expectancy is rising, but people recoil when faced with the higher premiums needed to keep their national insurance systems afloat.

Healthcare offers just as gloomy a picture. Health budgets are on the rise as the costs of medical and pharmaceutical research grow, as do public expectations of the service the state should provide. A revolution in social thinking is afoot as it dawns on the whole of Europe that generous healthcare, pensions and other strings to the social safety net can no longer be assumed as a birthright. More people will have to make private provision for things that their parents took as a right from the state.

But surely Europe is not slipping towards poverty? It must just be spreading the wealth inefficiently. Alas, no, for expenditure forecasts make disturbing reading. When the Commission launched its social Action Programme in November 1988, as foreseen by the Social Charter, Europe was riding high. The programme predicted unemployment would fall from 8.7 per cent in 1990 to below 7 per cent by 1995, as 6.5 million new jobs came on stream. Growth and stability were the watchwords, but by autumn 1993 unemployment had risen to 11 per cent as recession gripped the entire continent. Sixteen million people were out of a job, including one in five of Europe's citizens under twenty-five years old. Government spending began slipping out of hand.

Clearly Europe can no longer keep on as though nothing has happened. We must look again at the Social Charter and the action programme stemming from it, both of which were launched when times were good, but which we can no longer afford. Stable, high employment must remain our overriding priority, but experience shows that employment goes hand-in-hand with growth – new jobs begin to appear about six months after recovery and growth have taken off. Our efforts must go towards promoting and sustaining growth as the most steadfast job-creator of all.

I have no instant panacea to bring Europe's jobless back to work. But I would propose a two-pronged strategy of increasing investment in training and developing a more flexible labour market policy. These measures, together with the two proposed in the previous chapter – reducing tax and social burdens on producers and designing policies to bring the unemployed back into the habit and practice of work – will give Europe the adaptable, versatile workforce it needs to beat the recession and tap the lucrative markets of the future.

Making the most of our human resources

Education and training have changed beyond recognition over the last twenty years, and the distinction between them is beginning to blur. Gone are the days when our schools would pack our sixteen- or eighteen-year-olds off into the working world in the belief that they had learned all they needed to survive and succeed. Grooming children for employment needs to begin as early as twelve or thirteen, the moment they start taking the decisions that will determine the pattern of their working lives; and that grooming process should continue through vocational training and lifelong learning right up until they retire.

This is not a battle-cry to Europe's schools and universities to abandon the humanities and focus on narrow, job-specific technical training. Ancient Greek might very well be an appropriate beginning for a child destined to write computer programmes. Young Europeans need an education which gives them the wit to run machines, not to have machines run them. Learning must teach them how to adapt, to reason, to think ahead and, indeed, to learn. Only then will they be ready to exploit vocational training, turning ideas into markets and technology into prosperity.

This all needs money. In all too many countries, teachers are demoralized by low pay, low status, dismissive parents, suspicious politicians and a press hungry to find a scapegoat for the upsurge in child delinquency. Both teachers and trainers deserve pay and conditions commensurate with their responsibility and comparable to other qualified public servants. Intelligence, experience and education are a worker's three most marketable qualities. We can do little about the first, and the second comes with time; to treat the third as anything short of top priority is to commit cardinal folly against the future.

Yet there is frequently a disjointed quality to education systems in Europe, as though the steps from one level to the next were too high for all but the most determined pupils to take. As a result, *l'échec scolaire* – the school drop-out rate, as it is less elegantly called in English – has reached unacceptable proportions. Children lack incentive to keep learning, not just through poor parentage but also because the qualifications they achieve do not carry them smoothly up from one educational grade to another. Ideally, education would be a seamless ascent from kindergarten to university and beyond into the working world, for which people would be perpetually trained and re-trained. It should also be easier to join the educational flow at any level, whether you are a school drop-out with second thoughts or a mature student in search of a fresh qualification with which to launch a new career. *L'échec scolaire* feeds off the notion that once out, it is too late to get back in. The University of Teesside, where I am Chancellor, makes great efforts to encourage mature students in and to push them up the scale; some of Europe's more established educational foundations could learn a few lessons; Oxford, Tubingen, Salamanca and the Sorbonne take note.

There is an equal risk of abandoning streamlining in order to keep students in the system through the use of meaningless educational 'targets'. The last French government decreed that 80 per cent of pupils would pass their school-leaving *Baccalauréat* exam by the end of the century. (The French social journal *Futuribles* suggests that the idea evolved after a schools inspector learned during a visit to the Japanese car-firm Toyota that all workers on the production line had passed their school-leaving exam. He was so impressed that he relayed the message to the French government, and the 80 per cent target was born.) Anecdotal evidence aside, the point is clear: political targets are worthless if they merely lower standards. Or to use an athletics metaphor: if pupils are trained better for the high-jump, then targets may make sense; but if the cross-bar is lowered to ensure that more pupils manage to jump over it, there is little point.

Training is becoming less and less of an optional extra and more of an indispensable element of corporate strategy. But a crucial link is missing from the training 'industry': while training standards are growing steadily, the back-up of analysis so badly needed to lock firms on to the right kind of training is still in its infancy. Europe needs to build a market place of vocational training, with skilled forecasters offering independent advice on clients' training needs, in order to broker them into the appropriate training programme to meet their long-term business goals.

If a small firm wishes to build a production line, the manager goes to the bank for a loan, to the architect for a building plan, and to the accountant for advice on how to turn the venture to profit. But to whom does he turn for advice on training his staff to bring him such profit? Most probably only to the man who will end up doing the job for him. The employer needs as solid a return on his investment in his staff as does the bank manager on his loan. Soft advice from trade associations, Chambers of Commerce and other quasi- or non-governmental bodies is not enough; today's companies need a whole new, competitive industry in training.

The European Union has a major role to play in encouraging developments in this direction, but very rarely will it be appropriate to use legislation to do so. Drawing on the best practice across Europe, making comparisons, disseminating information, prodding governments, seeking consensus, and spending some money on studies and pilot projects: those are the best ways for the Union to have the biggest impact on the vital problem. Attempted coercion will only lead to resistance and a backlash.

Enabling the labour market to respond to employment needs

It is a sad irony about developed countries that dole queues and job vacancies should exist side by side. It would be utopian in the extreme to dream of a labour market where the right person for the right job was there waiting to snap it up the moment it became vacant. A labour market of such fluidity would, in fact, be self-defeating, stripping people of the incentives to work hard and well in order to build a long-term career, improve their living standards and even put down roots in a particular neighbourhood. Utopia aside, there must be a happier mean than that which exists in Europe today. Unemployment is still dogging virtually every politician on the continent, and yet I hear from employers the length and breadth of the Union that they simply cannot fill posts with the right people. What is going wrong?

First, there is a serious mismatch between skills and jobs. Our training market currently cannot keep pace with the needs of business. So great is the pace of industrial change that there is the risk of the task altering even before staff are fully equipped to perform it. This is a dreadful waste of resources. Secondly, the relationship between employer and employee also needs rethinking. Unfortunately, labour relations in many countries are adversarial at the best of times, doubly so during a recession. Those who support a restrictive labour market policy argue that at times of unemployment the employer wields excessive power, for it is his market. Society, they say, must step in to prevent exploitation.

This is an understandable reaction, but a flawed and counter-productive one, for a recession needs flexibility, not rigidity, to cure it. As unemployment soars, Europe should not be feeding it with a welter of rules safeguarding workers from the 'abuses' of temporary contracts, part-time jobs and shift work. For one, there is no compelling evidence to show that you can create jobs by curbing such 'atypical' work. Analysis in the Commission's 1993 Employment Report suggests, for example, that in the Netherlands, 'atypical' work is commonplace, but has no negative impact on overall levels of employment. And in the United States, the services sector has acted as a buffer during industrial recession partly because it accommodated so many different forms of atypical work.

There *is* evidence, however, to show that many full-time posts evolve out of temporary contracts. This naturally reflects an employer's desire to test the water before committing himself to creating full salaried jobs. The hesitant manager of a small company on the brink of expansion might not take the plunge at all if dissuaded by rigid terms of employment, and nothing other than his own commercial judgement can affect his choice. While large corporations can afford to offer securer terms of employment, smaller ones cannot. And small firms will become even more important in tomorrow's economy than they are today.

Social legislation, by virtue of its very existence, can have a deterrent effect on companies choosing where to invest. It may have few teeth, making little change to labour practices, as is the case with EU rules on maximum working hours in some European countries. But even without teeth it can still prey on the minds of company strategists. One might argue that they can lump it, or that they are oversensitive, or that an economic system which so spoils firms for choice is rotten to the core. But in free world markets they *do* have that choice, and the only way to strip them of that choice is to close up the market itself; and the closer world markets converge with each other, the fewer places there are for companies to take shelter, and the tougher they find it to survive. More often than not it is survival, rather than naked lust for corporate profit at the expense of workers' welfare, that managers have in mind when choosing to invest where labour laws are less restrictive.*

Perverse though it may seem, there are occasions when it takes the Union more nerve *not* to legislate than to legislate. Labour relations are a case in point. Numerous interest groups pile on pressure for protective labour laws as a windshield against growing competition from within Europe and without, or to stop the European Single Market becoming a playground for big business, as some wrongly perceive it to be. Governments themselves risk losing votes unless they act conspicuously to safeguard hitherto protected industries as they stagger unshielded into the single market place. Europe needs to steady its nerve and resist that temptation.

This does not amount to climbing down. Some of the Union's most resounding successes in the social sphere fall short of binding rules. Take the early years of the Community's Poverty Programme, or the pilot projects under the PETRA initiative to help youngsters make the leap from school to work in the late 1970s. The Poverty Programme has launched forty-one pilot projects through which European countries exchange experience on homelessness, the incapacity to find training or work, and people's inability to tackle bureaucracy. It will now go further, offering advice on illiteracy, the marginalization of unskilled labourers, and the exclusion of ethnic minorities and the disabled. In addition, EU programmes enable governments to share forecasts on the cost of social security in the future.

When the Treaty of Rome calls on the European Commission to 'act in close contact with Member States by making studies, delivering opinions and arranging consultations', it is not just shying away from rule-making; it is saying that Europe is a mosaic of such social diversity that its nations need to pool their ideas, expertise and experience long before pooling their sovereignty.

* This is not to say that the EU has no duty to fight worldwide for the defence of social rights: see pages 150–51.

Protecting the environment

The pollution of the planet has mushroomed since the economic regeneration of post-war Europe began, and public concern in Europe has mushroomed with it. Environmental degradation has burst upon us with such speed and ferocity that not even the founders of the Union, who were far-sighted enough to ban sexual discrimination at work, foresaw the need for Europe to protect its environment collectively through the Treaty of Rome. Perhaps they thought pollution would never reach epidemic proportions, or that if it did it would not affect cross-border trade, or at least that European countries could contain it themselves. Forty-odd years later, the idea of purely national controls seems faintly absurd; rules to curb anything from acid rain to nuclear waste are proliferating at international and pan-European level. But is it working?

Alongside social policy, environmental protection is arguably the most emotive aspect of government. It is also one of the newest, and its results are thus highly unpredictable, for we have little long-term experience against which to gauge the effects, and side-effects, of our actions. At least we have a few decades of medical expertise to tell us how car fumes damage our lungs; but we can only guess at what it takes to mend a puncture in the ozone layer. Because we are now acting to patch up our environment so fast, we will inevitably score a few mishits that damage other policy areas, notably those affecting trade. There is a growing risk of legislative overlap at national, European and world level which will hinder rather than help the fight to save the environment. As degradation spreads, we should be asking ourselves not only what to do, but whether it is sufficiently researched, whether it will have the desired effect, whether it impoverishes others, and above all who should take the action in the first place.

Efforts to save the environment will sink or swim depending on how thoroughly they address two key issues. First, there must be agreement on who makes and enforces the policy; secondly the policy itself must dovetail neatly with other fundamental objectives, notably the encouragement of growth, prosperity and employment through stimulating world trade.

On the first point, the European Union has a headstart over the rest of the world. As the environment does not feature in the European Community's founding Treaty of Rome, European governments have been obliged to agree unanimously every time they take concerted action to protect the environment. Consensus was required, and a considerable degree of it was found, for example on the conservation of wild birds, the treatment of hazardous waste, the protection of ground water and the reduction in air pollution. By learning to speak in unison, therefore, the Union has given itself a more forceful voice on the international stage and in many cases it is now taking the lead in the struggle to set world standards, for example against the depletion of the ozone layer.★

However, in recent years the European Commission is perceived by many to have gone too far. In the past, it won government support for directives on drinking water, even though differing standards of drinking water do not hamper cross-border trade, and on bathing water, even though this is only a transnational issue in so far as effluent from one country washes up on the beaches of another. Even in the Single European Act, designed to propel Europe towards a Single Market and restore the momentum of European integration, governments still refused to hand over the reins of the environment to the Community as a whole, except in

★ The EU has agreed to introduce curbs at least as strict as those in the Montreal Protocol, which calls for a ban on CFCs and most other ozone-damaging substances by 1996.

cases which jeopardize the Single Market, or unless they decide unanimously to act together.

The Single Market objective has itself clashed with the environment on several occasions, and not always of the EU's own making. However laudable environmental protection may be, it will do as much harm as good if it seeks to push other policies out of the nest. Germany's packaging law is a case in point. It is wholly admirable in its objective of reducing waste by encouraging the recycling of consumer packaging, but it has caused unfortunate side-effects, demonstrating that there are times when it would be better to lobby for rules at European level rather than taking the law into one's own national hands. Germany's packaging law, dubbed the *Töpferordnung* after German environment minister Klaus Töpfer, requires retailers to take back packaging from their customers, and decrees that at least 72 per cent of packaging for products sold in Germany should be recyclable. Germany's main recycling agency, Duallessystem Deutschland, then retrieves the packaging from the retailers, recycling it and selling it on. By sticking a 'Green Point' label on their products, manufacturers can assure their retail clients that they are obeying the law. As manufacturers from other countries have found to their dismay, no German supermarket will touch your produce if it does not carry the Green Point, since it would have to organize the recycling or re-use of the packaging itself.

This worthy law has created a vast 'waste-paper mountain' in Germany, causing a glut in Europe's burgeoning garbage market which the Duallessystem agency is now flooding with cheap waste paper. At first sight, that may be no bad thing; but as it is subsidized, German waste paper is undercutting recyclers elsewhere in Europe, discouraging new ones from setting up, jeopardizing local jobs and making a mockery of efforts to educate people across the continent to recycle their paper. Moreover, strict waste disposal laws have caused

Germany's recyclers to send their most troublesome waste abroad, provoking an outcry in France, where German hospital waste has ended up in shallow landfills reserved for hazard-free refuse, because nobody knew it had come from outside France.

In the case of German packaging, the motive was right, but the solution misguided. Only through far more rigorous, dispassionate analysis can we find the right solution and enforce it at the best level. For that process to succeed, the Union should apply four principles every time a green issue prompts calls for action:

– It should carry out a full cost-benefit analysis on all the possible alternatives. For example, when the Commission proposed maximum nitrate levels permissible in water, it decreed a sharp reduction in the amount of manure or chemical fertilizer used by farmers. This would have made vast tracts of farmland instantly uneconomic. Subsequent analysis proved it to be unnecessary. The same protection levels could be achieved in other ways, for example by taking account of natural de-nitrification in reservoirs, or by blending drinking waters from different sources. A proper cost-benefit analysis at the outset would have led to less draconian and equally effective rules in order to make drinking water safe.

– It should ensure the public is fully informed of the likely effects of action, and of inaction, and the alternatives it has ruled out and why. For example, EU rules on the transport of hazardous waste pose a series of crucial questions: should it travel by road, rail, canal or air? Who should be informed, just central government or regional and local authorities as well? Who should issue the permits? These questions are all of legitimate interest to a public worried about the risks of spillage.

- It should study all possible side-effects. Will the new measure impose an unsustainable economic burden on any especially vulnerable region, country or sector of society? Will it lead any of Europe's trading partners to lose business, and retaliate as a result? In the German packaging law mentioned above, for example, as well as EU rules that will almost certainly follow, lawmakers should explore possible side-effects and ways of preventing them.
- Does it demand a solution at European or international level, or could national or regional bodies tackle it adequately on their own? In other words, does it pass the subsidiarity test? For instance, is it the EU's job to regulate town and country planning when local bodies can do so themselves? Why should countries or regions need European legislation to make them explain the impact of roads and factories on the local flora and fauna, when local or national legislation would do just as well? The EU's own Environmental Impact Assessment rules exist, but do we really need them at European level?

The temptation for the Union to intervene in an ill-advised way is specially strong when dealing with emotive issues, notably the environment. It should be firmly resisted. Over the last few years the European Commission has become a last resort for action groups dissatisfied with their governments' perceived disregard for the countryside. The building of major highways in England, the Acheloos dam in Greece, or the Murraghmore Visitors' Centre in a beauty-spot in Ireland, all became test cases of Brussels' resolve to crack the will of governments determined to push ahead with developments which they saw as necessary in the local context, but which were reviled by many elsewhere in the Union. Some saw Brussels as a long-awaited *deus ex machina*, others as a meddlesome pest.

In each case, European action to stop those developments *might* have led to a cleaner environment, but it would also have upset the national balance between environment, transport and economic growth that each country must choose for itself. To shed national decision-making in favour of Union action just because Brussels may produce tougher standards is to fall in with a dangerous, centralizing logic that will provoke a popular backlash in the long term, even though it may seem 'better' for Europe's citizens in the immediate future.

On the other hand, pollution began defying national borders long before Europe even dreamed of removing them for its citizens. Joint action across the continent is indispensable, to curb acid rain and oil slicks, for example. But environmental controls themselves carry a health warning: environmental protection measures can cause serious damage to trade, if used deliberately or unwittingly to block out imports. Denmark, for example, forbids sales of beer in cans whether made locally or imported, only allowing re-usable bottles, a measure which has led to discrimination against foreign beer companies.

Europe needs to be as vigilant beyond its borders as within them if it is to detect disguised trade barriers. The United States, for example, has developed a canny knack of bowing to green pressures and protecting its domestic industry in one fell swoop. The so-called 'Gas-Guzzler' tax, imposed on the purchase of fuel-rich vehicles ostensibly to curb carbon dioxide fumes, in fact hits a suspiciously high percentage of imported cars.*

---

* This is done by using a system to calculate the amount of tax to be paid which is based on car fuel consumption averaged over the total sales by each manufacturer within the United States. So Chrysler or Ford can set off their big petrol-thirsty cars against their small run-abouts, and end up paying little or nothing. But importers, and particularly European firms, cannot – for most of their smaller cars are sold outside the United States and thus cannot be counted.

The US ban on tuna is a more graphic illustration of the dangers of mixing green issues with market protection, and of trying to export your environmental policy abroad in the process. Yellow-fin tuna, which swim in the Eastern tropical Pacific, congregate under shoals of dolphins. While trapping the tuna in large, purse-shaped nets, fishermen tend to catch the dolphins by mistake. The plight of the dolphin, already a star performer in zoos and soft-drinks advertisements, has captured public sympathy in the United States with ease. A vigorous campaign to save the dolphin has led to a ban, under the US Marine Mammals Protection Act, on all imports of tuna caught using 'dolphin-deadly' fishing methods. Moreover, countries which process such tuna and sell it on to America in tins are also hit under a so-called 'secondary' ban. Tuna fishing nations now face the insurmountable task of demonstrating, ahead of every season, that they will not accidentally trap more than 1.25 times as many dolphins as do American fishermen. The latter are inefficient by world standards, but their market share has rocketed since the ban. It is no accident that the European tuna-fishing fleet (mainly Italian, French and Spanish) is in crisis, while the US fleet is comfortable and expanding. A truly noble cause appears to have been hijacked by the murkier objective of protecting America's fishing interests.

It is often the case that pollution controls follow environmental disasters. The UK's Clean Air acts followed the disastrous smogs of the early 1950s, in which hundreds of people died because of a severe slump in air quality. At European level, the Seveso disaster just outside Milan led to an absolute requirement for proper emergency safety plans in all factories making or handling dangerous chemicals. It is alas often only by experience that we learn the error of our ways and start to correct them. But over time, Europe has learned that regulating companies is a balancing act between condoning naked abuse of the environment on the one hand and suffocating wealth creation and competitiveness on the other. Europe must never forget it is still walking that tightrope.

This may mean binding rules are necessary to stamp out misuse or careless handling of lethal substances. European Union countries need blanket rules imposing rigorous controls on the transport, use and disposal of toxic chemicals, particularly in the nuclear field – and we have such rules. The Union has laws governing the exposure of workers to dangerous physical, chemical or biological substances. It also has rules on the transport of dangerous waste and tight controls over civil nuclear matter, including rules on the transport, storage and sale of radioactive material as well as human exposure to it.

Where substances cause long-term deterioration but not immediate danger to people and their environment, the Union should abide by the 'polluter pays' principle. Take carbon dioxide, for example. Identical emission limits for all companies big or small, old or new, would certainly clean the air, but they might drive viable firms out of business too. Older companies need longer if they are to shed their polluting technology without raising prices, shutting down production and losing customers. Alternatively, you could let industry regulate itself, setting guidelines and penalizing companies that broke them. But here, the bigger fish could absorb the fines and continue to break the rules.

If correctly implemented, the 'polluter pays' principle would ensure that companies footed the bill for the damage they caused. To achieve this, every stage in the production chain would carry an environmental price tag, building the pollution into the cost of each production stage. Companies would calculate pollution in terms of cost, the ultimate deterrent. Damaging fuels, for example, would cost more than cleaner ones, encouraging restraint both from the energy producer and the energy consumer. And where pollution occurs, the bill should always work its way back up to the offender. It is a strategy which does carry risks: the polluter may have covered his tracks carefully, and to find him could cost the end-user dear in legal fees as successive intermediaries pass the buck further up the production chain. But it would be fairer on companies, kinder to the countryside and more respectful of the market place.

Agriculture

Agriculture is the part of Europe's economic heritage with which the greatest number of people still identify. It has inspired more heated debate than any other issue, and in some countries it carries an emotive weight way beyond its contribution to the economy. It has polarized North and South, free trader and protectionist, villager and city-dweller, rich and poor. It is Europe's *enfant terrible*, neglected by some countries, mollycoddled by others, a potential prodigy who stubbornly refuses to venture into the wide world on his own.

It also has more European laws round its neck than any other policy area. The drystone walls that snake across the Pyrenees, the Dolomites or the Yorkshire dales present a pastoral idyll with a whole network of Union support measures behind it. Europe's patchwork of small farms paints a pleasing picture of rural life, but also one of heavy subsidy, for it cannot survive without the aid on which it has relied for so long. Very few people would really wish that heritage to disappear. The only question is how best to maintain it.

Agriculture is far more than a factory for producing food. It is the tissue on which the fabric of rural life is woven, and as such cannot be subjected wholesale to the laws of the market place. The city-dweller can be cruelly dismissive: farmers have had it good for too long, and should be left to go under if they cannot produce food cheaply enough. But the deeper you go into the countryside, the more you realize that in most cases farmers are not a privileged social set, riding high on subsidies and cocking a snook at the free market. They are the caretakers of a dwindling community bitten by hardship and often deprived of basic services. There are fewer rural shops, post offices, buses, schools and jobs than ever before. A farm which employed ten men in 1950 might support just one worker now. The countryside as we know and love it simply could not survive without keeping agriculture at its heart. The Union's duty to bring that agriculture closer to the market place without consigning rural life to the history books will present the biggest test of all to its stewardship of Europe.

Against this backdrop, the much-derided Common Agricultural Policy has in fact served Europe well. Productivity is high, food prices are stable and the Union is self-sufficient. Prices are above world levels under the CAP, but they are not excessive, and the proportion of household income spent on food has dropped since the CAP was formed in 1950. No major industrial economy opens its doors to food imports at world prices, and Europe still gives less support to its farmers per head than either Japan or the United States.

And yet for all the expense of the CAP, we have still not ensured for our farmers as decent a standard of living as that enjoyed by those who produce goods or provide services. We have driven them into a vicious circle of over-production by subsidizing them the more they grow. The more they produce, the more the EU has to buy back into storage, and the less the EU can afford to pay per tonne if it wants to minimize the burden on the taxpayer. This has depressed farmers' incomes and driven them off the land. Technology has only made it worse: far from boosting Europe's competitiveness on world markets, fertilizers and sophisticated seed propagation have pushed EU farm spending higher and farmers further into debt, forcing Europe to erect bigger trade barriers to keep out imports. CAP spending has soared, yet the beneficiaries are still leaving the land in droves.

Rural depopulation is rising dramatically, both causing and reflecting disintegration: as people leave the land, the amenities leave with them as they become less viable to sustain, and other people therefore follow suit. Those who remain blame the government for deserting them; farmers clashed violently with the government on the Plateau de Larzac in South-west France in the 1970s and early 1980s, violence re-erupted over CAP reform in 1991, and further demonstrations took place over the GATT in 1993. Even in the cities it arouses surprising emotion. Some 80 per cent of Frenchmen live in urban areas, but many still consider France a nation close to the soil.

Europe cannot reverse the trend for fewer people to be employed in farming, but it can help render the process more palatable and encourage other acceptable forms of employment in rural areas. Governments are sometimes far too half-hearted in their efforts to encourage alternative industries out of the cities, and to nurture other sources of employment in the countryside. The greatest tool with which to soften the decline, however, has to be the CAP itself.

As a result of the major reform, which was achieved after great struggles in 1992, the Union is now helping farmers to survive on the land by topping up their incomes with direct subsidies instead of supporting them to produce more and inflating EU spending even further. This so-called 'direct income aid' is the main thrust of the reform package, and together with its additional incentives to protect the environment, it is a thrust in the right direction, for it will help build the kind of safety net farmers will need to weather the storm. It will also benefit shoppers when prices drop to market levels and farmers seek to produce value-added foods of higher quality, cashing in on the economies gained as crops and livestock shift to land where they can be farmed more efficiently.

But it does not go far enough, particularly in relating spending to the environment. As public awareness of farm spending and environmental damage grows, the use of the land will have to become more accountable to the citizen. Taxpayers will demand that a healthy slice of their money goes towards creating an improved countryside, with fewer chemicals and fertilizers, more planting of forests and more hedgerows, and a return to extensive rather than intensive farming.

Moreover, can direct income aid, just like the runaway production subsidies it is designed to replace, continue for ever? Are we not creating an even more artificial system than before? Do we not risk turning Europe's farmers into curators of museums tilling the land in order to gratify urban nostalgia for the countryside? By being paid to over-produce, at least they *feel* they are creating wealth for Europe, even if they distort markets and inflate taxes in the process. To tackle this dilemma, we need to look first at the alternatives. On the one hand, Europe could do nothing, allowing an already highly artificial production and sales system to persist, antagonizing the taxpayer and the rest of the world even further. On the other hand, Europe could open the floodgates of agriculture to free competition more swiftly, unravelling Europe's rural fabric practically overnight and fuelling social unrest right down to the tiniest hamlets.

There is, indeed, a risk that direct income aid could simply amount to putting off the evil day when farmers will have to leave the land. I believe that we need a solution which is at once radical and realistic; in the full knowledge that their income aid will not last for ever, farmers must be given the means to trade their farming assets in for a different life in a different job. In 1993, Professor Stefan Tangermann, from

Göttingen University, suggested that income aid should go to farmers in the form of a saleable 'bond', and only to those currently on the land. The size of the bond would reflect the past output of each farmer, combined with an estimate of the profit he would be making if the present system continued. Such a bond would have a healthy impact economically and psychologically: each farmer would know the aid was finite, focusing his mind on the need to gear himself for a new career; and it would give him the financial backing to find new work, and in good time, for he could choose if and when to leave the land, selling the bond in order to tide him over until he was established in a new line of business.

It would be a one-off lump-sum, which although costly would put an end to increasing support measures in the future and bring no new incentives to increase farm output. Instead, it would help heal the sclerosis currently gripping Europe's agricultural markets: it would loosen up the trade in farm property, lowering land prices as more farmers began buying and selling 'Tangermann bonds', making it easier for new farmers to start up in viable areas of agricultural production. The sheer finality of it, although hard for farmers to digest at first, would in fact encourage them and their governments to tackle Europe's farming future today, before it is too late.

So great is the level of depression among Europe's farming communities that they tend to treat the urban view of the countryside with resentment and derision. While city-dwelling ministers are busy taking decisions adversely affecting agriculture, other townsfolk pour into the country at weekends to marvel at their idyllic rural heritage, admiring the view but lamenting the loss of flowers and hedgerows, and then leaving gates open as they return to their secure urban livelihood. This is obviously an exaggerated portrayal of the farmer's eye view, but it does reveal a serious perception gap that can and must be narrowed.

The taxpaying public must continue to support a significant slice of agricultural land, accepting that it may also be used for non-agricultural purposes; if they prefer drystone walls to barbed-wire fences, they must be ready to pay for their upkeep. Likewise, farmers will strengthen their own case for support if they tune in more closely to public concerns. People do *not* want to turn their countryside into a rural museum; they want it to produce healthier, tastier foods, perhaps even organically produced, and to keep its forests, meadows, riverbanks, footpaths and habitats in better shape. People are as weary of the long-running battle between farmer and environmentalist as the farmer is himself. They see that the city can kill off part of the human soul, and they do not want it to happen to their children. A farmer I know in England regularly treats coachloads of city children to fresh milk, warm from the cow, and finds them gripped, if a little daunted, by the prospect. This is not to patronize the farmer, nor to coerce him into quasi-touristic activities in order to protect the rural environment. It is merely to explain that people want farming to adapt, not to disappear, and that the farmer should listen closely to public opinion, for it may be his best ally in the fight for survival.

Helping the poorer regions and countries catch up

The Union exists above all to help Europe's citizens help themselves. This must be the guiding light in Europe's agricultural reform, diverting aid to farmers to help them fend for themselves in future. In fact, the principle is just as apt when applied to countries and regions as to individuals, and needs pursuing with even greater vigour when large sums of money are involved.

The European Union is legally bound, under the Treaty of
Rome,★ to help Europe's poorer regions catch up with their
wealthier neighbours – an obligation reinforced under the
Maastricht Treaty. Leaders have set aside a major slice of the
EU budget – some 176 billion ecu over the next six years –
to help the Union's less developed countries and regions (in
particular, Spain, Portugal, Greece and Ireland) boost their
economic prosperity up to the Union average. These countries
suffer from being far away from the hub of Europe's Single
Market, and all except Spain are having to evolve at break-
neck speed away from near-total dependence on small-time
agriculture. Spain, Portugal and Ireland are slowly catching
up, Greece has yet to do so. All four vitally need the means to
build efficient plants and better roads to make and sell higher
quality products. If companies are to sink or swim in Europe's
Single Market, it is only fair that Europe helps its poorer
members to learn to swim first. It is also, as it happens, in the
interests of the richer members to help build up the markets
for their products.

The 'cohesion' countries are not the only ones to benefit.
Scotland, Southern Italy and some other regions enjoy special
funding, while larger parts of Europe's industrial heartland
also receive cash to attract new businesses and reverse industrial
decline. Whatever the region or however large the funding,
Europe's determination to close the wealth gap between
its regions is rich in potential, but fraught with dangers.

Europe's cohesion fund came into being because the richer
nations, with more than a little prompting from their poorer
brethren, foresaw the dangers of advancing from a common
market towards a common currency without giving Europe's
less developed economies a helping hand. It is an expression

★ Article 130a of the Treaty, amended by the Single European Act,
says: 'The Union shall aim at reducing disparities between the various
regions and the backwardness of the least-favoured regions.'

of political solidarity, and enlightened self-interest on both sides, which if applied correctly will help Europe to grow more harmoniously, but no less competitively, than before.

The money must be carefully spent. The European Union must define the beneficiaries and set the conditions more rigorously, ensuring that local authorities are capable of spending it well, and indeed of spending it at all. In fact some countries find spending EU money surprisingly difficult. By the end of 1992, Italy had committed under two-thirds of the money allotted to it for training and regional aid for the 1989 to 1993 period. The EU must ensure that the money genuinely restores the health of local economies and companies within them, setting them back on their feet rather than providing them with financial crutches. It must be a stimulus to economic reform, not a shield against it.

It must also dovetail with Europe's policy on state subsidies. Any Single Market needs a single set of rules on assistance given to industry by public authorities, be they national, regional or local. Failure to do so would reduce industrial 'competition' to a test of who can best twist the arm of the state into bank-rolling them. That is why the European Commission rigorously controls the amount of money that governments or regional bodies can deploy in order to lure companies to invest on their territory, thus preventing the race for investment from spawning beggar-thy-neighbour policies. And it is being far stricter than before on the richer regions of Europe in order to prevent them getting a better deal merely because their treasury has the money. It is a curious irony that firms investing in Germany receive just as much aid as their counterparts in Portugal. The Portuguese state is allowed to pay three-quarters of the cost when a company invests on its soil, while Germany can only pay far less, yet Portugal cannot afford to meet the ceiling while Germany can.

The overall aim of the EU's curbs on regional subsidies,

both from its own budget and from national treasuries, is clear: if EU subsidies overlap with those paid by regional governments which then trip over each other to attract outside investors, valuable money will be wasted, and Europe will be an altogether less attractive place to invest in in the long run.

Conclusion

When the six founding nations of the European Community sketched an outline of the Union they wanted to build, they relied on history and vision, but they were not clairvoyant. They knew roughly how the overall construction should look, but could not envisage the exact shape of all the rooms and the corridors between them. Since then, Europe's nations have converged incrementally, pooling new policies as new pressures bore upon them. The overriding need after 1945 was to house, feed and prevent renewed war between Germany and the allies, giving rise to the restructuring of the coal and steel industries, followed by the Common Agricultural Policy. Then came the need to tackle environmental destruction on a grand scale. Finally there came the push for a Single Market, flanked by calls from some for rigorous social laws to give workers as well as businessmen the fruits of prosperity. As several less advanced nations joined the EU, the need then arose for redistribution of wealth with their richer partners. Then came overspending which, together with recession, prompted the need to prune some of those expensive policies heavily, notably agriculture. Europe's short post-war history has been characterized by a steady stream of new, competing priorities all jostling for pride of place. The Union's primary role, as steward of Europe, is to marshal those priorities and restore the balance between them.

This leaves the Union with some awkward decisions. Calls

for tougher measures to protect workers, the environment and the 'cohesion' of richer and poorer regions are pitted against the overriding need to restore industrial competitiveness. The rapid disappearance of rural communities is cutting against the urgent need to reduce EU spending and enable agriculture to fend more for itself. The Union is called upon to adjudicate, whilst under pressure to withdraw from policies in the name of subsidiarity.

The Union might be tempted to bury its head in the sand, opting for emollient compromises rather than radical reforms, as it has done at times in the past. It would be wrong to do so now. The greatest challenge of all – Europe's lagging economic performance – must be a compelling priority when the Union assesses new social laws and reassesses existing ones. Social policy must be turned round to focus on equipping the workforce to attract and exploit future business, while making unemployment as painless as possible within that constraint. All social provisions need judging by their impact on our ability to compete, and the Union's action programme itself needs serious review, beefing up the positive measures while discarding those that genuinely burden business. When taming pollution and curbing environmental damage, Europe as a whole needs to agree a better analysis of who should be doing what, between the regions, governments and the EU itself, if it is to act more effectively. It must weigh up the pros and cons of action and inaction more rigorously, taking special care to avoid trampling over trade both within Europe and with the outside world. On agriculture, the Union cannot shy away from further reform, but what it can do is give farmers a future, plus the means to prepare for it well in advance by converting their past toils into a tradable ticket for a future career. In all sectors, it is the steward's job to usher in the future, not let Europe dwell excessively on the past.

Europe and the Wider World

When I was asked once at the Institut d'Etudes Politiques (Sciences-Po), one of France's élite educational establishments, whether I was a European or an internationalist at heart, I said I considered myself to be both. There is no inherent contradiction in being European and international, and in my case British for that matter, when it comes to economic and trade relations between Europe and the wider world. Putting Europe first is wholly compatible with a commitment to global free trade, because global free trade is what is best for Europe. Creating the best environment for companies to thrive within Europe should go hand-in-hand with a commitment to open trading and investment rules on a worldwide basis. The danger comes if Europe, or any other trading bloc, raises the perimeter fence around its market merely to protect its companies from the perceived threat of outside competition. Europe's top priority must be to create the climate most conducive to the growth of its economy beyond Europe's borders. If, in its eagerness to nurture its companies, it builds a hothouse of protection around them, they will be starved of the oxygen they need to thrive in world markets.

Introversion would be no better for Europe's economy now than it was for Europe's governments in the past. The examples of countries foundering as a result of isolationist policies far outnumber those where they have flourished. The open market policies of South-east Asia bore fruit while protection in Latin America led to stagnation and debt. The

Latin American countries have now taken courageous steps to reverse this trend by opening up their markets to each other and to the outside world.

That does not mean all forms of protection should be ruled out, for Europe, like its competitors, has the right to defend itself against any abuse of internationally agreed rules of trade. But the more that protection appears to go beyond lawful self-defence, the more likely it is to spark a backlash of retaliation and counter-retaliation. And the stronger those international rules become, the less likely the abuse and the greater the trust between trading partners. That is why the European Union has consistently supported the greatest free trade arbiter of all, the General Agreement on Tariffs and Trade, as one of the central pillars of its foreign trade policy, and why we insisted so strongly that the Uruguay Round should result in the establishment of a stronger, more authoritative successor to the GATT in the form of the World Trade Organization.

Global interdependence

It is no accident that this chapter on relations with the rest of the world focuses particularly on economics. Economic policies are more important to international relationships today than ever before. The removal of the Soviet threat is a clear illustration of this: since the collapse of the Soviet Union, its erstwhile enemies have hurried to help Russia and its former satellites build their markets, stabilize their economies and sell their products abroad. In the past, a united Soviet empire spelt danger which needed matching militarily. Today, a poor, disintegrating Russia is a far greater threat than a confident, stable and prosperous one. Last year's elections in Russia showed that the victory of moderate democratic forces to the East is still fragile. As the world shrinks and borders open, it is in every country's best interest for its neighbours to be rich, confident and eager to do business.

Global economic interdependence is not merely a new, indigestible piece of jargon devised to replace the language of the Cold War. It reflects hard economic facts. The European Union buys and sells one-fifth of all goods traded worldwide. Our exports to the rest of the world are equivalent to almost one-tenth of our gross domestic product. Twelve million European jobs depend directly on the export of goods. European companies are particularly prone to invest outside their own country, too. OECD estimates show that EU countries account for over half of all OECD outward investment and more than 60 per cent of inward investment. Europe, therefore, has a specially strong interest in allowing trade to flow freely across national borders.

There are those who bow to these facts but still say the European Union should turn away from world markets and focus on its closer neighbours instead. Whilst important, this overlooks the fact that Union countries export far less to the rest of Europe than they do to the world beyond.* The bulk of EU exports goes to countries which are further away or with which we do not have close formal links. Furthermore, our fastest growing long-term markets are in Asia and Latin America, not Europe.

Europe is also trading more and more with the developing world, which already buys almost half of our exports. Most surprising of all, the third world will have matched the first world in economic performance within twenty years, according to medium-term forecasts. Even with the present levels of competitiveness the Union's exports to the developing world

* EU exports to the nations of the European Free Trade Association, Eastern Europe and the Mediterranean basin, as well as to the ACP grouping mainly of former African, Caribbean and Pacific colonies, together account for just 43 per cent of all EU exports.

could grow at over 5 per cent a year (in volume terms) for the coming decade, since the latter have been growing at over double the rate of the industrial countries, and are expected to sustain these growth rates. As their economies expand, the poorer countries of the Southern hemisphere will look further afield and with increasing technical sophistication for new markets, diminishing their unhealthy dependence on their wealthier Northern counterparts. The North–South divide will finally begin to dissolve, largely, though by no means only, because of trade.

And yet Europeans do not always react to the irrepressible globalization of the world economy with the boldness and vigour that it requires. Nowhere is this clearer than in our relations with Asia. A handful of relatively small nations in South-east Asia have rapidly grown into the most dynamic motor for economic growth in the world. Europe's consumers have given their cheap, high-quality goods a rapturous welcome, but many of Europe's companies are recoiling in fear, lobbying governments for protection rather than fighting back by competing on price, quality and service. The 'Tigers' of the Far East are to be kept at bay rather than challenged either in Europe's markets or on their own soil.

Spurred on by Japanese and American investment, the economic miracle in Asia is spreading beyond Taiwan, Hong Kong, Singapore, South Korea, Thailand and Malaysia. It is engulfing Vietnam and, most telling of all, China. China's economic reforms over the last fifteen years are yielding spectacular dividends as the country registers a real growth rate of over 10 per cent a year (as high as 12 per cent in 1992), the highest in the world. Europe continues to focus on the traditional transatlantic economy, but the United States is gradually diverting its energies to Asia. Although undoubtedly grounded in fact, and boosted by the media attention paid to last autumn's summit in Seattle between members of the Asia Pacific Economic Cooperation group, the 'Pacific Rim' is primarily a clever logo designed to make America feel part of the Asian miracle.

Statistics bear witness to this miracle: by the end of this decade, trade in the Asia–Pacific area will outstrip trade within the EU. The output of the average Asian worker is doubling every ten years, while Asian (and predominantly Japanese) banks hold almost a third of the world's official reserves and foreign currency assets. Asia even has demography on its side: by the end of the century the number of twenty- to forty-year-olds will increase by 80 million while it will decline in Europe and the US, greatly enhancing Asia's capacity to produce, buy and invest.

The newly industrialized economies of Asia also account for most of the sevenfold increase in outward investment by the developing world in recent years. Much of this is to China, Vietnam and other low-cost countries in the region, but some 7 per cent of it has come to Europe, according to the OECD. If Europe continues to regard Asia solely with suspicion, it will suffer incalculable harm as a result.

Establishing open markets worldwide

Europeans are so busy taking sides in the oversimplified debate between free trade and protectionism that they risk missing the point altogether. Europe can sometimes sound to an outsider like some strange battleground from the Dark Ages. The British would accuse the French and their 'Latin' allies of building a fortress against marauding speculators, while the French would retort that the 'Anglo-Saxons' and their British 'Trojan horse' were turning Europe into a continent 'exposed to the elements' of free trade, a continent which let in foreign goods like a 'sieve'. Britain threatened to hold up EU integration altogether if France blocked the

GATT over farm subsidies, Germany peered awkwardly across the Rhine, and common sense vanished temporarily into the mist.

Not even the most ardent crusader for open markets would claim it is a cost-free policy, nor that it is a panacea for all economic ills. Like democracy, it is merely the worst form of economic policy except all those other forms that have been tried from time to time. It is a moderate, not an extreme creed which calls for a careful blend of innovation and regulation if it is to function fairly and foster competition without suffocating the industries it aims to serve; but it is above all an active, not a passive creed, and nowhere is this clearer than when dealing with foreign markets. Europe must set an example at home by removing the final barriers to its Single Market and ensuring no new ones are erected in their place. It must then fight equally hard to secure access for its goods and services abroad.

It is tempting to resort to retaliation to open foreign markets, but this is profoundly flawed. The sorry experience of the United States' 'crow-bar' trade legislation bears this out. Since its introduction through the 1988 Omnibus Trade Act, the Super 301 law has enabled US congressmen to oblige the President to retaliate against protectionism abroad by closing America's borders to imports from countries that fail to open theirs. However, far from always prising foreign markets open, this much-vaunted crow-bar has sometimes encouraged America's trading partners to clam up, seriously undermining countries' attempts to join forces and tackle tomorrow's trade issues in a united fashion.

In principle the idea of a 'global cop' to reform trade rules is an attractive one, but no individual country should be entitled to assume that role. We should instead come together, as we have increasingly done, to strengthen the international institutions designed to do the job. In this way we can set the rules and ensure fair adjudication if it is alleged that trade rules have been broken, but no international institution short of a world government can actually physically enforce the rules. That is why the international system has to allow national governments (or the EU) to defend themselves if the rules have been clearly broken. But it is clear that the stronger the GATT and other such bodies become, the less its members will be entitled to take the law into their own hands, and the less they will be tempted to do so.

Quite apart from the fact that neither the GATT nor any conceivable successor is going to have the effective power of a world government, even in the limited areas of trade, some of the most influential trading nations in the world, notably China and Russia, have yet to complete their current negotiations to join. Europe must keep a careful hold on its existing trade armoury for the foreseeable future, using it in ways permitted by the GATT and working to strengthen the GATT's own fair trade rules in the meantime. Europe's right to defend itself against trade abuses from outside is not only compatible with its commitment to open world markets; it actually enhances it, as it encourages our partners to take our efforts at world liberalization all the more seriously.

The European Union locks itself periodically in a heated debate over the trade weapons it has and how it should use them. The European Commission, which runs the EU's trade policy with the outside world on behalf of its twelve member states, is frequently criticized for failing to defend European industry against 'cheating' by its foreign competitors: Japanese videos, Chinese bicycles, Brazilian steel, Romanian fertilizers and a host of other products have indeed been 'dumped' on Europe and deliberately sold for less than they cost to produce in order to capture large slices of the European market from the EU's own fragile producers. Some argue that Europe needs stronger weapons with which to fend off such practices, while others say the Commission should have fewer qualms about using its existing weapons more frequently.

There is indeed compelling evidence that Europe is the victim of predatory pricing policies by firms hunting for new markets abroad. It is important to be clear why such practices should be regarded as unhelpful, and not just the normal result of energetic competition. This explanation is a simple one. In an open competitive Single Market it is not normally possible for there to be such significant differences of price. Market forces would ensure that prices do not significantly vary from one part of the market to another. Indeed if there were growth discrepancies alarm bells would be ringing and the competition authorities would soon be hunting for wider cartels or other restrictive practices. In international trading, however, there is no overriding competition authority and indeed no guarantee that barriers and restrictive practices would be absent. That is why trade policy has to operate as a surrogate for competition policy, and seek to ensure fair trading conditions where there are clear distortions of the market.

When predatory pricing policies are pursued, most though by no means all of the perpetrators tend to be exporters of raw materials from the developing world or manufacturers of technologically sophisticated consumer goods from South-east Asia. (There is equally strong evidence that many of them enjoy high subsidies and other forms of government-spon-sored protection. In some countries, the state still partially controls much of the economy, setting prices and bearing the costs of electricity, property depreciation, even wages, and other running costs normally borne by the company itself in a free market. These measures can impose on European firms a distinct competitive handicap, especially when combined with an aggressive export policy.)

The fears of European industry have been further fuelled by developments closer to home. As Communism crumbled and the Russian rouble lost its purchasing power, the artificial trading links between the Soviet Union and Eastern Europe began to fray, leaving large, unwieldy companies desperately grappling for new markets. Naturally many turned to the European Union which had just absorbed one of their biggest trading partners, East Germany, and where demand for cheap raw materials was high. Imports of some products, such as aluminium and steel, began flooding into the Union at a time when the recession was biting hardest at the EU's most labour-intensive traditional industries.

Many European firms now harbour great resentment as a result of such events. They argue that they have been cutting costs and sacking workers only to see their markets swamped by unfairly subsidized products from abroad. The chorus of support for the Union to build itself a bigger armoury of weapons has grown even louder over the last few years. This bitterness is understandable against the backcloth of recession, but it runs the risk of seriously missing the point.

Trade defence weapons are not only compatible with a global commitment to free trade; they can actively enhance it, curbing abuse and encouraging our partners to take us more seriously when negotiating the further removal of trade barriers through the GATT. But Europe already has considerable powers to stem the flow of imports and punish abusive export practices. It uses those powers fairly and efficiently, although further improvements are now being sought. These powers fall into three main categories, all with the blessing of the GATT.

First, the Union can impose 'anti-dumping' duties on out-side companies which have deliberately exported at prices below the cost of production, increasing their share of the European market at the direct expense of their European competitors. In such cases, the Commission is alerted either by a complaint from a disaffected competitor, or from its own contacts with industry, or even in some cases by reading the newspapers. If there is sufficient evidence at the outset, the Commission will launch an inquiry. The Commission will send a team of investigators to the suspected company's headquarters and go through its books with a fine-tooth comb to analyse whether it is deliberately depressing its prices in Europe to boost its market share. The same team will then visit that company's competitors in Europe to assess whether their share of the European market has dropped simultaneously.

If, for example, you are a manufacturer selling computers to Europeans for far less than they cost to make, and for far less than you are charging your domestic customers, and your European competitors have seen their sales plummet over the same period as a result, you are likely to be accused of dumping. You may be ordered to pay a duty to make up the 'dumping margin' and restore fair competition. More probably, on the advice of your Brussels law firm, you will promise to sin no more and set minimum prices of your own. The Commission's provisional decision will then be extended, amended or scrapped by the full Council of Ministers no more than six months later.

Secondly, powers, known as 'countervailing measures', are available to offset the government subsidies that the offending companies may have enjoyed at home while pursuing their market-hunting activities in Europe, because when it comes to state subsidies, the world is patently *not* a level playing field. Such subsidies are no less damaging to fair trade in Europe than those paid contrary to Union rules to European companies themselves, and the Commission pursues both types of abuse with equal rigour. Europe has set the pace for the rest of the world to follow in its drive against subsidies, which damage long-term prosperity wherever they are.

Europe would be shooting itself in the foot if it were to treat over-subsidized companies from outside the Union any less harshly than one of its own.

Thirdly, the Union can take emergency action to safeguard its markets in the event of a sudden, massive upsurge of imports in a particular product, as we have witnessed recently from Eastern Europe, Russia and some of its former satellites. The Commission will investigate the complaints, but not necessarily the accused companies themselves – for 'safeguard measures' exist to stop temporarily any sudden change in trade flows damaging European industry irreparably, rather than to punish any deliberate malpractice by its competitors. These measures, too, are permitted under the GATT rules. They are measures designed to have a temporary effect, not to prevent change brought about permanently by normal competition.

To ask whether these three trade weapons are powerful enough is to ask the wrong question. Their effect, both actual and as a deterrent, depends not on their calibre but on the will of their owners to pull the trigger. The European Union's anti-dumping, anti-subsidy and safeguard rules are as solid on paper as almost any others among its GATT partners, if Europe's member governments have the political will to use them.

It would be a more pertinent question to ask whether these weapons are used with sufficient accuracy. The Commission already has a good eye for detecting trumped-up charges from European manufacturers merely seeking shelter from foreign competition. Indeed, it throws out most of the complaints it receives. It abides carefully by the GATT rules, and consults widely with industry and government experts before taking decisions. These rules will be improved following a decision by EU foreign ministers in December 1993 to make Europe's trade defence more efficient and more accurate.

First, the Commission will work to tighter deadlines,

deciding whether to open an inquiry no more than a month after receiving a complaint, and finishing it no more than eight months later, thereby halving the current time limit on investigations. This will reduce the damaging uncertainty that hangs over companies while they await the outcome. To enable it to do this, the Commission will be provided by the member states with more staff. It could then split the investigators into two, one half assessing dumping and the other analysing the damage caused to domestic firms. This will help produce faster, fairer conclusions.

Secondly, a greater right of appeal to the courts will reduce the risk of political influence, which gives all trade defence rules a bad name. The EU's Court of First Instance, created to relieve the overburdened European Court of Justice, could become the forum for such appeals. It has the capacity to handle the extra work.

In addition, I believe the investigators should do a thorough analysis of the effect of any defence action on European consumers. It is the customer who pays the immediate price of the EU's anti-dumping or anti-subsidy actions, for the cost of the 'dumped' goods will rise on the shelf, either as a minimum price or as a surcharge. The consumer deserves to be reassured that he is paying in the short term to ensure fairer market conditions in the long term, not just to keep less efficient European companies in business. If the price paid by the consumer is too high, the anti-dumping complaint should not be upheld. Looking at the consumer's interest is possible under the present rules, but it needs to be more clearly legitimized and more effectively practised.

Fourthly, and most importantly, Europe will enjoy stronger GATT rules, for the GATT is our best defence against unfair treatment of our own exports. For example, when faced with the threat of exclusion from the American market, European industry has frequently offered to cut its exports through a 'gentlemen's agreement' with the Americans instead. European steel was forced into one such so-called Voluntary Restraint Agreement for ten years with the US. None the less, as soon as it expired the American steel producers tried to get penalties imposed for precisely what had been done under the agreement. Admittedly Europe has used similar devices, running VRAs on cars and video-recorders from Japan, and on textiles from Turkey. Fortunately, VRAs and other so-called 'grey area' restrictions will be phased out under the Uruguay Round, and the sooner they go the better, for they are opaque and often reside on shaky legal foundations.

Above all, a stronger GATT will improve trust. It will be harder for one trading nation to take the law into its own hands to open another's market, and harder for a bilateral dispute to escalate into retaliation and counter-retaliation. It will be harder to subsidize industry at the expense of competitors, and harder to bend the anti-dumping rules to appease powerful lobbies. That is the kind of trading system the world's ever more interdependent economy demands.

Social justice

As global economic barriers fall and transport becomes faster and cheaper, companies are freer to pick and choose where they manufacture their goods and employ their staff. This means that European-based multinationals need no longer choose only between local towns or nearby countries when deciding where to set up new factories: they can choose between continents. They follow ever more complex criteria in deciding where to invest, and countries use ever more sophisticated means in the fierce struggle to attract them on to their soil.

This has fuelled the row over 'social dumping', provoking

one of the most confused and over-simplified polemics in the history of trade. A company that leaves country A for country B where the labour is cheaper is deemed to have 'dumped' unemployment on country A. As more and more companies shift their production facilities to poorer countries, some say Europe is being unfairly penalized for looking after its workers and its environment; others say the over-rich, over-regulated West is finally getting its comeuppance. Some say the third world should be forced to bring its social security up to Western levels, while others say just the opposite: we must dramatically reduce our own labour costs if we ever want to compete again. One man's 'exploitation' has become another man's 'comparative advantage'. The debate has grown excessively polarized as people take sides according to their ideological hue, denying this crucial subject the dispassionate and rigorous analysis it deserves.

To call what happens 'dumping' is unpersuasive. Dumping means selling goods at artificially low prices, and it is hard to believe, and frankly impossible to prove, that poor countries are deliberately depressing the levels of social protection in order to gain a competitive edge in their bid to attract outside investment. More plausibly, high social protection has become an increasingly prominent political objective in Europe as national wealth, and organized labour, have developed over the decades. Developing countries have not acquired sufficient material prosperity to entertain such levels of social protection. For them to seize their competitive advantage and use it for all it is worth is not a form of cheating. Those countries currently on a lower rung of the development ladder cannot be accused of deliberately denying their people a decent wage and working conditions merely to steal jobs from more socially 'civilized' countries. And, of course, as they rise up the ladder they are replaced by others below them; there is already evidence of production shifting from Asia to Eastern Europe, for example.

But the legitimate use of economic advantage must be distinguished from the abuse by any country, developed or developing, of universally recognized human rights: slavery, bonded labour, child labour, harassment of labour representatives and the denial of fair labour treatment to racial minorities. Such abuses certainly occur with alarming frequency. It is Europe's duty to fight against them, and we do. We address these issues in all bilateral relations, we are active in the International Labour Organization, and we are taking a lead in preparing for debate on this problem in World Trade Organization next year. More must be done. But the aim must be to work by dialogue and aid, not by coercion. Any action must be proportionate to the abuse and, above all, it must have the proven effect of making the situation better, not worse.

Take the harrowing subject of child labour. There are some countries so underdeveloped that the alternatives may be much worse. Who is to say that a child forbidden from working in a Bangladeshi textiles factory will go to school instead rather than take to the street? Schooling may not even exist, and his parents may be so poor that they cannot look after him, and need his paltry wage to help the family survive at all. We are right to encourage Bangladesh to structure its society better, and to help it do so with the aid that we give, but in practice it can only build up its economy if it is allowed to produce and export cheap textiles. At least in the short term it may be impossible to do so without employing youngsters who might otherwise be left on the streets to starve or beg.

That is an extreme example of the moral dilemma that social and environmental conditions in less developed countries may present. None the less, there are cases where child labour, even adult labour, falls little short of captivity and is a clear breach of human rights, however much allowance one may make for appalling economic pressures. Many of the most shocking accidents could be avoided through proper safety enforcement in factories and other worksites. Europe should spare no effort in pushing for worldwide rules that ensure basic minimum protection against the abuse of human rights in the workplace. Moreover, we should support the International Labour Organization and other multilateral bodies in this process. There may even be extreme cases where trade instruments are justified; but, in general, trade policy itself should not be used to achieve those laudable objectives, and any tough action should be preceded by a rigorous analysis of the economic context in which the apparent abuse is occurring, and trade should be used to encourage, not to punish. Europe should actively encourage higher standards of social protection worldwide, but should stop short of trying to impose its own standards unilaterally on its trading partners: we have suffered too much from such unilateralism on the part of others.

In any event, social protection alone does not make a country uncompetitive. A worker who receives high wages, long holidays, generous maternity leave and a good pension may still be comparatively productive if he or she is highly skilled, well educated and works in a country with high capital investment, good infrastructure and a strong emphasis on industrial research. Social costs are an important factor in a nation's competitiveness, and in Europe this is an issue that needs urgent attention. But just as it would be a mistake to ignore this factor, it would also be a mistake to regard it as the only one that matters.

Europe owes its falling competitiveness at least as much to the rigidity of its own economy at home. Europeans are less prepared to change employer, function or location than their counterparts even in other developed countries. And we spend far too little on industrial research and development: just 2 per cent of GDP in 1990, as against 3.4 per cent in Japan.

The existence among other trading partners of low-wage economies is in fact good for Europe's economic health, not least because they spend much of their foreign exchange on buying Europe's exports. Western Europe now sells more to Eastern Europe than it buys even though its trade barriers are lower than ever before, as the nascent democracies of the East thirst for high-tech goods. Such a trend can create new export-related jobs, which are comparatively well paid. And our exports to Latin America and the dynamic new economies of Asia, including China, have risen by over 10 per cent a year since 1990, while sales to Japan and North America have dropped over the same period.

It is ironic that as fears rise of Europe 'exporting jobs' as its companies invest overseas, it has been 'importing' them at a growing rate. EU overseas investment virtually doubled in the second half of the 1980s, but investments made in Europe from abroad increased five-fold. As the creation of the European Single Market approached, multinationals rushed to set up shop inside the new Europe, partly to exploit new business opportunities but partly also to avoid being left out in the cold, just in case Europe should turn into the fortress that some feared was being created. The mere anticipation of a large new market has brought a rush of investors into Europe. The Union has reacted by doing everything possible to ensure that companies sink their roots deep into the local economy, employing local staff, sub-contracting local firms and actually manufacturing – rather than merely assembling – high-technology products on European soil. This includes so-called 'screwdriver' rules to prevent non-European firms from merely assembling products from parts imported from abroad in order to side-step European anti-dumping restrictions.

This is wholly legitimate. Once you have lured a company on to your territory, it is tempting to impose 'local content' rules to ensure that it uses local jobs and local parts in the process; but to impose rules of this kind can be self-defeating. That is why in the Uruguay Round we sought to have rules reinforcing fairness in the use of trade-related investment measures, or TRIMS, to stop the GATT countries from offering excessive rewards, or imposing excessive demands, on companies looking to invest on their soil.

Inward investment has done little, however, to quell fears that European jobs are flooding abroad. Critics say Europe is losing its value-added production, and importing more and exporting less as a result. This is a simplistic view of events. One major French company told me in 1992 that as it was unable to compete for a huge electrical switchgear contract, it began producing one of the components abroad. It won such a large deal that it had to install new production lines back in Europe to meet the soaring demand.

The popular belief that European companies produce goods in poorer nations merely to sell them back more cheaply into Europe is also fundamentally flawed. Over four-fifths of Europe's outward investment goes to other affluent members of the OECD, and less than 10 per cent to Latin America and the newly industrialized Asian countries. In fact, the success of the European Single Market as a magnet for investment has prompted fears that outside investors will choose Europe instead of developing countries.

Europe is too defensive in its approach to the interdependence of the world economy. Statistics are not enough to remove ill-focused fears that our economy is fraying because we let jobs slip away to poorer countries that do not play by our rules. And even when statistics are used, it is often to expose the plight of one product or industry without looking to see just how much Europe is winning overall from the same open markets. As markets change, perception must change too, and I believe that process is already under way. How many Europeans, for example, still dismiss Japanese cars as a cultural invasion? They realize that European car manufacturers are becoming more and more deeply involved in cooperation with their Japanese counterparts, and that the car industry is growing increasingly multinational.

Worldwide relationships

On the other hand, to believe that nations will one day forfeit all their preferential trading links with each other in favour of one set of world rules would be too naïvely optimistic even for Voltaire's Candide. The world trade map is a mosaic of national groupings, some clustered together and others spread across the globe. Some are linked by geography, others by history and almost all by economic self-interest. These ties have grown up for differing reasons but, having done so, they will undoubtedly stay until replaced by a 'best of all possible worlds' of perfect global rules enforced by trusting governments and respected by law-abiding multinationals. A worthy goal maybe, but for the moment at least, a touch unrealistic, and going well beyond the current GATT objective.

Preferential trading relationships arise, for example, when groupings such as Europe want to encourage trade with and the development of countries with which they have particular sympathy. The Lomé Convention was an early example of this. It reflects a desire on the part of the Union to assist and encourage trade with countries in Africa, the Caribbean and the Pacific which had in many cases been colonized by European countries and for which a special sympathy continued. Much later on the so-called 'Europe agreements' with the countries of Eastern and Central Europe reflected the same basis of thinking.

Preferential trading relationships will never go completely, nor should they. It can be easier, for example, to remove barriers between two or a few countries, especially when they are neighbours, than to remove barriers multilaterally. So long as this does not lead to the *raising* of barriers towards the rest of the world, the net effect is beneficial.

The European Union is the prime example of deep 'regional' economic integration, and more besides. Lesser regional trade experiments are proliferating throughout the world as nations seek influence, and safety, in numbers. Canada, the United States and Mexico are building a North American Free Trade Area, with common trade, labour and pollution standards; Poland, Hungary, Slovakia and the Czech Republic have formed the 'Visegrad' group to compensate for loss of trade with post-Communist Russia and stake out the path to eventual EU membership. Thailand, Malaysia, the Philippines, Singapore, Brunei and Indonesia are contemplating turning their ties through the ASEAN group into a fully fledged ASEAN Free Trade Area, to be finalized in the first decade of the next century, providing a counterweight to Japan's overwhelming economic influence in Asia.

The European Union has its own panoply of special ties. The Lomé Convention has already been mentioned. In addition, the European Economic Area (EEA) is enabling Austria, Finland, Norway, Sweden, Iceland and Liechtenstein to join Europe's Single Market while they ponder over, or prepare for, the deeper political links that the post-Maastricht Union will entail.

As people's lives become influenced more by decisions taken beyond their own borders, so governments grow bolder and more experimental in the forms of cooperation between them. The European Union is by far the most sophisticated such experiment in the world, while the European market is more united even than its American counterpart in many respects. It is now easier, for example, for a bank established in London to open branches in Greece, Portugal or Germany than for a Washington-based bank to do so in California or Alabama. Likewise, foreign manufacturers in the US must confront an obstacle course of some 100 testing and certification schemes, plus a contradictory array of technical requirements, before they can sell their products across all states. Civil engineers, too, must battle with a host of different codes of practice.

The more Europe sets the pace by knocking down its own barriers, the more influence it can have in shaping world rules, and also influencing those of other groupings. This is already happening: the Brussels Commission receives a steady stream of foreign ministers and officials seeking advice on how to remove market barriers with their neighbours. Even the United States has modelled NAFTA's government procurement rules almost entirely on those in force in the Union. Dangers arise, however, when by clubbing together, countries exclude others. The label 'fortress Europe' is wholly inaccurate, but it has none the less proved devilishly difficult for the Union to shrug off. America is anxious to avoid a similar name-tag being attached to the NAFTA agreement.

This risk of exclusivity is particularly strong with so-called 'hub and spoke' relationships, where outlying countries feed into a bigger market at the hub of a wider trading system. This can generate an unhealthy degree of dependence. By giving former colonies or other 'special' trading partners a back door into your market, you can dilute their incentive to buy and sell with their neighbours and with each other, as well as fuelling resentment elsewhere. The European Union's Eastern neighbours, for example, have been slower to open their markets to each other than to dismantle barriers with

the EU itself. It is a painful irony that after fighting Communism for so long, the West is urging the former Soviet
empire to restore the commercial ties that cemented it so
artificially before. And yet this is crucial if the Union is to
discourage Eastern Europe from swapping its excessive dependence on Russia for an equally unhealthy, exclusive reli-
ance on EU markets.

There is a further risk that trade preferences will simply
carry the imprint of powerful industrial lobbies rather than
reflecting sound economic logic. Why, for example, does the
US Administration feel the need to preserve double-digit
tariff protection for textiles or glass into the next millennium?
If Europe pays too much heed to the clarion calls of its
industry lobby, it risks deforming the economies of its trading
partners, particularly the poorer, less influential ones; countries
will seek to sell us what they know our industry will let us
buy, rather than the things they make best. Developing
countries, for example, pay far higher import duties when
selling furniture to Europe than when exporting raw timber.
By importing only what we cannot or will not produce
ourselves, we risk handicapping poor countries in their efforts
to diversify out of raw materials and into more sophisticated,
higher value-added products in order to widen their industrial
base.

Preferential access to Europe's markets must be based on
fairness and sound economic principles. We must reduce the
number of products with no preferences at all in order to
avoid the kind of distortion just referred to. We must also
encourage our partners to boost trade with their neighbours
and prevent too much dependence on Europe. And we must
build on the Uruguay Round by pushing for the total
reciprocal removal of as many tariffs as possible through the
GATT. This in turn will cause trade preferences to wither of
their own accord. In other words, to the extent that preferen-

tial arrangements, in spite of their advantages, have a distorting effect on world trade, the right approach is to weaken their impact by reducing tariffs all round rather than removing benefits from those to whom we have given them.

Obviously trade preferences have a political purpose too, which Europe should continue to exploit: Europe can offer market access to help stave off political instability and safeguard democracy, as shown by the EU's decision to respond to the storming of the old Russian Parliament in October 1993 by accelerating moves towards a more generous trade agreement with Russia; Europe can suspend market-opening agreements to dissuade governments from wavering in their commitment to human rights; and it can keep its doors more open to some developing countries than to others to avoid harming beneficial trade links established in colonial days, as it does through the Lomé Convention. But the goal must always be to enhance the long-term economic prospects of all of Europe's partners, for in an ever more interdependent world it is through this route that our own future prosperity lies.

The European Union's evolving market acts as a magnet for trade with Europe's neighbours further afield, drawing the continent into closer touch with the Mediterranean nations stretching round North Africa and the Near East to Turkey. But Europe's ties with the Mediterranean basin go well beyond trade. When the Mediterranean prospers, Europe heaves a sigh of relief, but when it suffers, the whole continent suffers with it. Our historical and demographic links are so strong that we have a special interest in developing relations far deeper than those with our more far-flung neighbours.

Turkey, Morocco, Tunisia and Algeria all have vast migrant populations working in Europe but maintaining strong family and other ties with their home country. Turkey, Cyprus and Malta all aspire to join the Union, while every single country bordering the Mediterranean, and many of their neighbours beyond, ply most of their trade with the EU. If the Mediterranean basin is Europe's 'backyard', then it must be our overriding objective to help make it a stable and prosperous place in which to live.

Europe is already rising to this challenge. Until 1996 1.5 billion ecu a year will be spent through grants and loans from the European Investment Bank on helping Mediterranean countries attract investment, export their goods, improve research, stabilize their energy supplies and protect their environment. In Northern Morocco, the Union has agreed to stimulate investment and discourage farmers from producing the cannabis which currently accounts for one-third of all drugs sold on the streets of European cities.

We have, then, to encourage the dismantling of barriers on a multilateral basis, while accommodating our need to maintain specially close links with particular areas for historical or present-day political reasons. But as trade barriers come down, other aspects of domestic policy which can be regarded as distorted competition come more to the fore and may even increase. Apart from differing levels of subsidy and environmental standards, which have already been referred to, are differing tax systems and changing currency values to be regarded as distorting competition?

How must Europe respond to these new challenges? Clarity, as ever, must begin at home. Europe must be clear on the competition, environment, exchange rate and other policies that best suit its own member countries before seeking to shape those policies worldwide. It must keep up a constant dialogue with its world partners. Global talking shops are frequently accused of achieving little of substance – even the GATT, which has real teeth, is dubbed the General Agreement to Talk and Talk – but that is exactly where the value of some of those fora may lie. Ministers will be more candid if they feel their words are transformed into minutes rather than laws which will one day bind their governments. Hence the need for international bodies which allow a continuous and uninhibited exchange of views. The Group of Seven, whose leaders, finance ministers and senior officials meet at least once a year, is the most prominent example. Yet all spontaneity has gone out of the G7 as its officials clock up record air miles meeting and drafting the final 'conclusions' months in advance. Its leaders pledged at their Tokyo Summit in 1993 to turn it back into a less formal, more confidential fire-side chat. I will believe that when I see it.

The Organisation for Economic Cooperation and Development, grouping the world's wealthiest democracies, is another good example of an international forum whose great potential is tempered by excessive stage management. Each year ministers sit down to a stodgy diet of each other's pre-cooked speeches on the situation of the world economy, rounding off with a pious declaration calling for more of the same cooperation as they called for the year before. Journalists pounce on any hint of a change, even though these generally reflect a textual compromise rather than any shift in policy. I was struck in June 1993 by how several ministers, speaking from prepared texts, glossed over the importance of maritime safety, without making a single reference to the oil tanker which had crashed on the rocks of North-west Spain the day before.

Scepticism and cynicism can go too far, though. The current proliferation of opinion-making bodies large and small, public and private, is basically desirable, for it facilitates the task of the decision-makers. The well-researched views of the OECD's various working groups, as well as position papers produced by non-governmental bodies, businesses, organized labour and academia, provide crucial back-up for the GATT, the International Monetary Fund, the World Bank, and other executive organizations. Unfortunately, the voice of the developing world is lacking from the OECD, a gap which other world bodies have not yet adequately filled.

Politicians are rarely honest enough to admit it, but the truth is that there is as yet no consensus on the answers that should be given to the new questions that have most recently come to the fore. Nor, when international agreement is needed, can any one country or grouping impose its views on the rest. That is why bodies which can rightly be described as talking shops may actually be indispensable. It is only through them that any consensus can emerge, but for that to happen the research, analysis and debate has to be clearly focused and organized. If it is, it is not too much to hope that there will be a gradual approximation of rules in such areas as competition and environment policy, which can at a later stage be formalized into international agreements.

This may seem like imposing a new layer of regulation, but the alternatives can be far more costly. In the aftermath of the Chernobyl nuclear disaster, for example, many countries imposed a total ban on foods with even the slightest trace of radiation. European exports suffered immeasurably, even though our food was pronounced perfectly safe by recognized and respected scientists. It took the Union months of negotiation to hack a path through these obstacles. The more countries learn to regulate in step with one another, basing their rules on fact rather than fear, the less trade will be lost unnecessarily.

Competition and environment policy

While competition, or 'anti-trust', policy may have been an American invention, the Union has been in the vanguard in developing it during the last decade. With some of the world's most highly developed rules for cracking down on cartels, monopolies and unfair subsidies, Europe is well placed to push for similar disciplines on a global scale. The need is greater than ever before, for fair competition at home can be stifled by activities initiated beyond the Union's borders.

The Union already acts against companies upsetting the balance of fair competition on its own market, irrespective of their origin. Tetrapak of Sweden, the world's biggest food packaging firm, was fined 75 million ecu by the European Community for systematically squeezing its competitors out of the Union market over many years. When the European Commission discovered that several chemical firms had met regularly in Swiss hotels to agree prices of polypropylene and keep off each others' customers, it was just as tough with the Austrians and Norwegians as it was with those from the Community.

Action of this kind is fully justified, but obviously penalizing non-European companies can generate considerable hostility, and so the more Europe cooperates with its partners to prevent conflict occurring the better. The Union now operates an anti-trust agreement with the United States, wider in scope than any comparable agreement anywhere in the world. The aim is to detect the impact of monopolies and cartels on each other's markets, forewarning each other of problems and seeking to defuse disagreements before they flare up. Yet even after consultation we may disagree on how to curb unacceptable company behaviour, and even on whether it is unacceptable in the first place. Harder still, we may not see eye-to-eye on whether it should be handled by the European Commission or by the Federal Trade Commission in Washington, or by both.

Unfair business practices, like pollution and crime, have less and less respect for borders, and we need international rules with teeth to catch them. This would not entail the wholesale surrender of all anti-trust powers to a global policeman like the GATT. That may be an admirable goal in the long run, but the world will not be ready for a long time. Forfeiting the right to fine companies, order repayment of subsidies, block mergers and prise open cartels would for most countries be unacceptable. Far better to agree a set of common principles through the GATT, leaving individual countries to enforce their own competition rules in a way which respects these principles. The GATT could then arbitrate if two nations failed to agree on whose rules should apply to a particular offending company, or if one country accused the other of violating the GATT principles themselves.

The GATT could define cartels, monopolies and other restrictive forms of business behaviour and industrial cooperation. All GATT members would render these practices unenforceable in any of their courts, but each country could pursue offending companies in its own way. However, there is a catch: GATT is an agreement between governments, not companies, but companies would be the ones more likely to break the rules. To resolve it, governments could solemnly swear to use their best endeavours to police companies operating on their market, preventing abusive behaviour where possible and punishing it where necessary. If they reneged on this commitment, others could challenge them through an impartial GATT disputes panel.

Similarly, the creation of a supranational authority to vet company mergers is sound in theory but utopian in practice. Under a more modest approach, all GATT signatories could agree common principles and sufficient procedures to enforce them. This would inevitably lead to squabbling between national anti-trust bodies vying to control mergers which straddle two or more countries. The GATT's mechanisms for settling disputes could arbitrate by offering an impartial analysis, weighing up the pros and cons of the merger itself and advising on which authority should handle it. It would be unrealistic to imagine governments letting the GATT actually *decide* the outcome until the whole world marches to one set of market rules – the European Union's governments are loath to let outside bodies tamper with the business plans of their treasured national 'champions', although economic logic demands a broader view. It is one of the successes of European integration that the member states of the Community actually agreed in 1989 to allow the acceptability of major mergers to be decided at European level, rather than by the governments themselves. None the less, when the Commission decided to ban the takeover of the aircraft maker De Havilland by a Franco–Italian consortium in 1991, the howls of outrage from France and Italy were of an unparalleled ferocity.

Global rules to protect the environment are growing just as indispensable as those to protect companies from each other. And yet this is a minefield of passion and prejudice in which almost every world action can provoke a chorus of anger either from sworn defenders of the environment or from those suspected of polluting it for their own profit. More dangerous still, the environment has become a rich-man-poor-man issue as the North seeks tougher environment protection in the South, and the South, in return, accuses the North of double standards, of seeking to impose rules on the South after it has enriched itself at the South's expense.

It is, nevertheless, imperative to write world rules to stem the serious degradation of the environment. If in the process we respond with passion rather than pragmatism, overlooking the myriad pressures bearing down on governments, it simply will not work. International rules must complement national environment rules rather than replacing them, encouraging countries to act together rather than taking the law into their own hands when dealing with their trading partners. All nations must work on a common diagnosis of global degradation before prescribing their own medicine for other people.

Rich countries risk falling into one of two traps when seeking tough action from their poorer counterparts. Firstly, they inevitably draw accusations of 'environmental imperialism'; we have despoiled our own natural heritage to get rich quick and are now dictating tough controls on poorer countries when they cannot afford it, threatening to close off our markets unless they comply. The developed world needs to act with restraint when seeking global rules, for any over-reaction will only encourage the accusers to dig in their heels. This should not stop tough action to prevent what is agreed on a widely accepted international basis to be a flagrant abuse of the environment, particularly when such abuse is obviously for short-term gain and long-term loss. There may even be times when third world governments would welcome dissuasive action from outside to reinforce their own efforts to control the offenders on their own soil. But the type of action needs more careful study than it currently receives. Is it right to ban trade outright, for example trade in ivory, when a controlled trade at high prices would capture the rarity value of culled ivory and divert the profits to African game management?

Secondly, heavy-handedness could make environmental problems worse, for anything which increases poverty will increase environmental degradation. The forests of Nepal are disappearing, risking further flooding in downstream countries, because people need logs to heat their houses; the elephant population of Zimbabwe is under pressure partly through poaching and partly because local farmers are encroaching on their territory, for they need more land than they would if their farming techniques were more efficient.

The World Trade Organization designed to replace the GATT should work out ways of taking account of the cost of improving or abusing the environment when fixing trade rules. Countries acting unilaterally to restrict trade for environmental purposes would be liable to pay compensation to traders who lost traditional business as a result; but where there was agreement that the restrictive action was desirable, trading partners would waive their compensation rights. This would count as their contribution to environmental protection.

This will require special rules for settling disputes. One solution would be to include such rules in all environmental agreements signed between two or more countries. Such multilateral agreements are likely to multiply in the coming years; any country which fails to build dispute settlement rules into its agreement would lose its protection under the WTO. This would not stop countries taking tougher action than that recommended by the international community. In cases where one country's action has a direct impact on another's trade, the latter should have the right to compensation, or in extreme cases to impose 'retaliatory' costs on trade from the former. Far from being an assault on national sovereignty over environmental policy, this would ensure that the cost of national initiatives falls on the decision-makers, not on their neighbours.

Ideally, all countries would agree on a series of environmental goals and on the trade tools to achieve them. If individual nations then chose to protect the environment on their own, they would risk provoking a rash of claims for compensation.

Europe must put its own house in order before seeking to shape international rules with any real degree of authority. The European Union is already fairly advanced down this road. Through the success of its barrier-free Single Market, the Union is now better qualified than ever to seek the removal of tariffs, duties and other trade barriers on the world stage. As it develops competition rules to stop companies digging up the newly levelled playing field on which that Single Market operates, it is well placed to seek similar world-wide disciplines. And once European governments have clearly identified the boundary between pollution they tackle together and pollution they solve alone, they can begin the task of helping to draw up world environmental standards too. These standards must encourage poorer nations to clean up without casting them further into poverty and thus into conflict with their industrialized partners.

This may seem quite a shopping list for a continent, indeed a world, gripped by recession and underconfidence. We must all steel ourselves, remembering that however exposed we feel in the process, open world markets are the way to promote growth, both to get Europe out of recession and to ensure further growth on a long-term basis.

Europe has the advantage of history: as small countries, the member states of the Union have always depended to a considerable degree on international trade, and since 1957 they have worked hard to build a solid barrier-free market between themselves. Hence our ability to cooperate fully in the negotiations on services and intellectual property within the Uruguay Round, where Europe was if anything readier to commit itself to liberalization than were the US and Japan.

The successful conclusion of the GATT Round also confirms the Union's ability to present a united front to the rest of the world. In the summer of 1993 we were accused of internal divisions and of protectionism, but since then we have shown vision, internal solidarity and consistency and have contributed those qualities to the GATT outcome. I am confident that Europe will continue to lead from the front in trade liberalization. We can show the way to more recently formed trade areas and work with other world economies to sustain and develop the world markets on which European industry depends.

CHAPTER 7

Common Foreign and Security Policy

Apart from the human casualties of the terrible war that has torn Yugoslavia apart, one of the greatest victims of the cross-fire in Bosnia has been the reputation of the European Union itself. While Vukovar, Dubrovnik, Osijek and other Croatian and then Bosnian towns were obliterated as the Serbs systematically stole land, European foreign ministers seemed to be condemning them more in word than in deed, imposing sanctions and talking of air strikes but stopping short of anything that would halt the Serbs in their murderous tracks. They sent in humanitarian troops, and men in white coats to monitor the countless ceasefires as they crumbled, but this seemed simply to become an excuse to refrain from firing back at the Serbs. The generation which created the European Community after the Second World War did so in order to stop anything like it happening again, and yet the first war to strike the continent since 1945 seemed to leave the EC floundering hopelessly in the public eye. When Maastricht was enacted, the irony seemed too painful for many people to bear: Europe had the gall to commit itself loftily to a 'common foreign and security policy' with which to face the world, while Sarajevo shivered and starved on the sidelines. Europe talked while Bosnia burned.

The frustration is wholly understandable, but to blame the European Union is misguided and dangerous. The former Yugoslavia descended into civil war because extremism broke the fragile peace between Serbs, Croats and Bosnian Muslims, and Europe and America, without a common line on tough military action, could not impose peace and were not prepared to try. Their reluctance was understandable. They had their own bitter experiences of seemingly unwinnable wars: those where the terrain is dense, the target hidden, moving and often intertwined with those you are seeking to protect, and where the roots of the conflict run deep into history. France learned painful lessons in Algeria, the United States in Vietnam and more recently in Somalia, and others elsewhere. All are now loath to enter such conflicts unless the exit is clear. Even in Ulster, Britain knows that, as in Bosnia, full-scale military engagement cannot keep neighbours from killing each other. In the Gulf War, the enemy was obvious, though daunting, while the terrain was perfect and the mission was clear; Bosnia was altogether different.

For the 'something must be done' school of thought, the European Union may seem fair game in the search for scapegoats over Bosnia. But they would be wrong, for the EU has never been responsible for Europe's security and defence. Admittedly, it was built to prevent war, but with only one tool at its disposal: the right to remove economic barriers in order to make traditional enemies too economically reliant on each other to fight. Such a tool might be needed for the republics of the former Yugoslavia in the very distant future, but it would clearly be insufficient right now, even if it existed.

NATO, not the Community, was entrusted with the task of maintaining peace in Europe. Indeed, it fulfilled the mission so well that the main threat, the Soviet bloc, crumbled. But the very nature of that threat – totalitarian military power – pushed the national, ethnic and religious feuds of Eastern Europe underground for over forty years. This made conflict in Europe unthinkable because of the balance of terror which existed between East and West. Now that the ideological arm-wrestling is won, those feuds are reawakening with a vengeance, above all in the former Yugoslavia. Neither the EU nor NATO has the experience or tools to tackle them.

The Cold War nuclear balance made both East and West increasingly cautious in their military involvements, as it became clear how easily a Suez, Vietnam or Bay of Pigs crisis could bring the world to the brink of destruction. But small military engagements did still take place and individual European nations did fight in conflicts, usually derived from their colonial past. Sometimes they fought those conflicts alone, such as France in Algeria and Britain in the Falklands. At other times they worked together with allies under UN auspices, like Belgian troops in former Belgian Congo. In most cases, those nations earned a high degree of solidarity from their EU partners, but caution over local disputes further inflaming East–West conflict as well as continuing differences in national objectives left no place for a united military response from the European Community as a whole. Sheltering beneath the NATO umbrella and united against one powerful enemy, Europeans remained independent-minded about their own smaller conflicts and, in the case of Britain and France, about their nuclear capabilities.

Nevertheless, European nations did gradually learn to cooperate over foreign policy, issuing joint statements on human rights, earthquakes, famine and local wars, meeting ever more frequently at official and ministerial level, but *without* forfeiting national sovereignty in order to take joint decisions on matters of foreign policy and defence.

Political cooperation between European nations grew up in the 1970s and was formalized under the Single European Act in 1987. EPC, as Euro-shorthand puts it, is a loose web of consultation between the twelve foreign ministries of the EU's member countries, with a secretariat in Brussels but no 'common' decision-making machinery as such. It began as little more than a talking shop, and has gradually evolved into a forum through which its members can align their policies, seek support for each other in times of crisis and, most importantly of all, help the European Union to exert its economic weight to halt military aggression. As a result, the EC was among the first to impose economic sanctions against Iraq for invading Kuwait, while bolstering the so-called 'front-line states' – Syria, Jordan and Turkey – with aid to compensate for the trade they lost through the sanctions. The Community then imposed a freeze on trade with Serbia and Montenegro in May 1992, tightening the belt around them in order to force the Serbs to negotiate.

As the Community continued to build on the creation of its Single Market by planning to converge its economic and monetary policies as well, the collapse of Communism in Eastern Europe forced a new imperative upon the EC's leaders: a single currency might make Europe an economic giant, but it would remain a political dwarf in the face of conflicts erupting across the globe as the Soviet empire splintered apart. In addition, there was a fear that Germany's economy could be drawn Eastwards unless it was tied 'politically' to the West. Hence the birth of the somewhat vague concept of 'European political union' alongside the plans for an eventual monetary union.

Europe's leaders did not foresee Yugoslavia, far from it; but they sought to match Europe's growing economic unity with an ability to take joint decisions on foreign policy and ultimately on defence, so guaranteeing greater stability on a continent racked no longer by the presence, but by the absence, of the Soviet Union. In the process it would also ensure that as the newly reunified Germany reawoke after forty-five years to the need for its own political voice in the world, it would be willing to speak through the European Union rather than by itself. Nobody expected that the capacity to take objective joint decisions could be created overnight. It was bound to be a slow process, but it would never come about unless the appropriate structure was set up to nurture it.

By the time European government leaders met at Maastricht to sign the new Treaty on political as well as economic and monetary union on 9–10 December 1991, it was already too late to save Yugoslavia; seven days later European foreign ministers reluctantly agreed to recognize Slovenia and Croatia. No blueprint for the future so late in the day would stop the subsequent bloodshed on the Union's doorstep. Indeed the timing was so poignant that many saw Maastricht as a charade, or a feeble attempt to exploit Yugoslavia in order to push for more centralizing EU powers, which Yugoslavia has shown could never work. Once again, the pro- and anti-European crusaders in almost every country donned their armour and engaged in a sterile joust about whether Europe *needed* to seek to bring together its twelve foreign and defence policies in order to prevent Yugoslav-style crises in future, or whether attempting to do so would *dilute* their ability to act individually, so eternally different were their views of the outside world. I would side firmly with the former camp, but I believe the debate deserves far more dispassionate analysis than it has received.

Why should we want one?

The most important decisions are always the hardest ones to reach. Obvious though it sounds, this lies at the heart of current opposition to the creation of a common foreign and security policy for Europe. If twelve ministers fail to agree on the maximum noise levels permitted from a lawnmower, they will not put the lives of our soldiers, friends, families, or even of our lawnmower salesmen, at risk. But if the Union's foreign ministers fail to act at all because they cannot agree whether our territory is under attack or our vital interests at stake, then we are jeopardizing our lives by allowing our ministers to share powers with the rest of Europe in the first place. For to attempt to reach a common approach may not only fail, but also hinder individual countries from taking action which might otherwise have been open to them. And it is infinitely harder to agree on troop deployments than on lawn-mower noise, a fact which strengthens the case of the sceptics.

Taking joint decisions on defence and foreign policy may, therefore, seem like a dangerous, unprecedented and irreversible surrender of national sovereignty, a leap into the unknown. And yet we are hardly starting from scratch. Europe's nations have fought tooth and nail down the ages, but rarely have they done so alone. European history is a patchwork of shifting, opportunistic alliances, as proud nations made friends of foes overnight if it suited their security needs at the time. Most were short-lived as the empires of the great powers jockeyed for supremacy in the nineteenth century. But they do show how ready Europeans have repeatedly been to trade national sovereignty in order to secure the best protection against a perceived threat.

Happily, the days of single-issue alliances, where one country would often befriend another only because both feared a third even more, have gone from Western Europe. The member countries of the European Union have now permanently pooled considerable security powers through NATO. Although they have only committed themselves to act within NATO territory and without forgoing the right to act independently if they choose, Western nations have been prepared to take this major step because Hiroshima and Nagasaki opened a new chapter in security: the ecological and financial price of war today would be so high that countries seek to avoid it at all costs.

Modern warfare is also harder than ever to ring-fence, for even if the fighting itself does not spread, the political repercussions almost always do. This in itself can help deter aggression, for when a spark risks becoming a bushfire, you are less inclined to light the flame in the first place. Like the wagon-trains of the old Wild West, nations now see their safety in numbers, warding off their aggressors with the threat that an attack on one is an attack on all. This is the cornerstone of the NATO alliance, whose founding Treaty of Washington states, in Article 5, that: 'an armed attack against one or more of them, in Europe or North America, shall be considered an attack against them all'.

Economically, too, defence and security cooperation can bring benefits. To be effective in modern conflicts, today's armies must be equipped and maintained with the most up-to-date technological weapons and information systems. These do not come cheap. So it came as no surprise that once the Berlin Wall crumbled, treasuries argued that the need to maintain such an expensive war machine had receded, and belt-tightening and burden-sharing became watchwords that echoed between NATO allies across the Atlantic. The much-vaunted Cold War 'peace dividend' was expected to bring if not instant then certainly substantial relief to the public purse. From Britain's 'Options for Change' programme through to the withdrawal of US troops from Europe, the results can be seen, but, as generals and admirals continue to remind us, we still need a sophisticated defence capability to combat a changed but still difficult threat. This defence will need to come increasingly through cooperation between European partners.

So the moral of modern-day defence is clear: the broader and longer-lasting the alliance, the stronger and cheaper each nation's defence will be. If most countries in Western Europe are already protected by NATO, then why do we need to expand the European Union's powers in order to cover foreign and security questions, risking serious institutional overlap between the two? After all, we might alienate

America, on whom NATO's success has depended. The two, however, need not be incompatible; just as the EU can and does exist alongside other economic groupings within Western Europe without hindering trade across the continent, so too can NATO and a security-conscious EU itself co-exist. As US congressmen lean quite legitimately on their President to slim down America's military presence in Europe and ease pressure on the public purse, the European Union, through the Maastricht Treaty, must and can gradually strengthen that European pillar.

The EU is not frogmarching its members into a reluctant defence union against the tide of history, far from it. European countries are bracing themselves for the future, searching for the institutional clothing that will match their economic size as well as the changeable political weather they know they will have to brave. NATO was the perfect outfit for the Cold War. Yugoslavia may be but the first of a series of smaller, less ideological but no less vicious conflicts to which Europe may have to respond, and neither the European Union nor NATO yet has the right gear to do so. Fitting the EU out will prove doubly difficult because its future size is unknown, so the gradual enlargement of the Union will have to be taken into account. Ironically, Yugoslavia has shown that public faith in the Union may depend on its ability to react to future Bosnia-type crises, yet that same public often tells Europe to keep its hands off defence. Europe faces a triple task: to learn to respond fast, effectively and in unison to world crises in the ensuing vacuum of post-Cold War politics; to keep its own people on board in the process; and to move in tandem, not at cross-purposes, with America.

Why have we not had one before?

To dismiss Europe's political cooperation so far as nothing more than a powerless talking shop would be a major mistake.

It has used economic sanctions to great effect against South Africa as well as Iraq. It has enabled Europe to sponsor peace envoys to seek a negotiated solution to the Yugoslav crisis, as well as to participate in the Middle East peace talks in Madrid in 1992. And through regular dialogue with the ASEAN and Rio groups, it has given Europe a common voice with which to encourage political stability in Asia and Latin America.

Despite its success, though, the European Union's political cooperation currently lacks bite. Europe has been unable to present a united military front under NATO auspices in Kuwait and Yugoslavia, the two crises which have dominated the early 1990s. In both cases, Europe managed to agree on 'soft' action – sanctions and emergency aid – undeniably necessary but stopping short of any joint use of offensive military force. In the Gulf, this did not stop Europe's major military arsenals – Britain and France – from linking up with Italy and Belgium to play a conspicuous role under the UN umbrella, restoring faith in the belief that Europe could still fight, even if not *en bloc*. But in Bosnia Europe really did lose face despite all of its exhaustive diplomatic efforts. It rejected all offensive military engagement, and did so right in its own backyard. Inaction may well have made military sense, but Europe did not emerge looking strong.

Europe remains hamstrung in its approach to 'hard core' military questions for two reasons. First, all conflicts since the Second World War have been either too small or too big to warrant a joint European response; that is to say, the threat of war has come either from conflicts 'local' to one European country – generally of an ex-colonial nature – or from the Soviet Union, which was too menacing for anything less than NATO itself to confront, and with weapons of mass destruction at that. Many of those 'local' conflicts risked sucking the superpowers in anyway, becoming ideological wars waged by proxy, for example in Angola, Mozambique, Afghanistan,

Nicaragua and even Vietnam. The Cold War turned the world into a giant powder keg which the smallest spark could set alight.

Secondly, Europe's own historical baggage left its nations at odds with one another, despite their NATO alliance. Territorially divided, riddled with guilt and constitutionally forbidden from controlling even its own defence, post-war Germany was incapable of taking the helm in Europe's quest for a common policy. Even forty years after allied victory in Europe and Japan, German reunification still reawoke old fears among Germany's partners. So what of the other potential founders of a European security policy? Britain was reluctant, preferring to ally itself with America as it came to terms with the loss of its former colonial might. Any defence measure that looked too exclusively European could in its eyes alienate the Atlantic alliance without which NATO would crumble. And what of France, a founder member of the European Community and a nuclear power in its own right? France was the most reluctant of all to countenance a collective European defence policy in the early days of post-war Europe – it was the French Parliament which in 1954 vetoed the creation of a European Defence Community, then considered to be the necessary counterpart to the European Coal and Steel Community, the precursor to the EC itself. In fact, France retained its nuclear independence, stood aside from NATO's integrated military command and even sent NATO's strategic headquarters packing across the border from France to Belgium. Such was the legacy of General de Gaulle.

Internal differences none the less never managed to dent Europe's ability to stand shoulder-to-shoulder with America and fend off a common enemy when such an enemy was clearly identifiable. But the global military map has now changed, forcing Europe to rethink its strategic objectives responsibly. As the Maastricht Treaty shows, that rethink is already under way as the European Union sees its international influence grow, and its post-Cold War defence priorities take shape.

Its first step is to respond to the United States' desire for partial withdrawal without losing them altogether. The European members of NATO must respond to American calls for greater 'burden-sharing' by relying more on their own military personnel and hardware to fill out NATO's defences. Europe should not mistake America's withdrawal as a desire either to turn in on itself or to shift its allegiance to Asia, for Washington is just as adamant that Japan should start taking on a defence role in the context of UN approved operations.

Paradoxically, the United States will feel more inclined to maintain its commitment to Europe if it knows Europe does not take US support for granted. Europe should actively avoid giving the impression that it wants Washington to forfeit its voice in the deliberations over Europe's defence. This would only encourage the belt-tighteners and the isolationists in Congress. And Europe will surely need America at its side just as much tomorrow as it has in the past. The prevalent US belief, for example, that Yugoslavia is 'Europe's war' has greatly impaired Europe and America's ability to forge a common stance on military, or even humanitarian, involvement.

Europe's and America's security interests may gradually diverge, but they will never part altogether; in local conflicts there will usually be a case for one side to help the other, and both will need each other's solid backing in the United Nations. For what now constitutes a national interest? Empires, thankfully, are finally out of fashion, being expensive to run and unpopular both with their subjects and with the world community at large. Borders need defending, but the best way to defend your border may often be to reduce its economic importance: frontiers are threatened less by aggressive military intervention than by immigrants in search of a job, and the most effective weapons to keep them at bay are trade and prosperity. These are global interests which Europe and America will always share, and they must cooperate persistently to achieve them.

So what does now threaten Europe's security? There is, it seems, currently little left to jeopardize Western Europe's own territorial integrity, but it would be foolish to take internal peace for granted; although largely a matter for governments themselves, social unrest is at its most intense for many years, and violent racism is on the rise.

The greatest threat of all, however, still comes from the East. That threat takes several forms, all emerging from the rubble of former Soviet power and the absence as yet of a new order to replace it. There are conflicts where existing republics dispute their post-Soviet borders, for example between Armenia and Azerbaijan; there are civil wars, where tribal or religious tensions reflect the past failure either to secure satisfactory borders or to achieve fair and lasting ethnic integration, notably in Yugoslavia, but also in Georgia. There is the perpetual risk that tough economic reforms will provoke social chaos and extreme deprivation, leading either to mass migration West or to an upsurge in crime – European police already predict that Eastern European drugs cartels may soon upstage Cali and Medellín as the greatest narcotics threat to Western Europe. There is also the risk of a defiant backlash by ethnic enclaves left stranded abroad as their country of origin is cut adrift. Bosnia is the most potent example of how vicious this backlash can be, but there is the even larger, though as yet less explosive, case of the Russians themselves. There are twenty-five million Russians living outside Russia itself, making up 42 per cent of the population in the Baltics, 38 per cent in Kazakhstan and 22 per cent in Ukraine. All discrimination, retaliatory or otherwise, against the Russians whom Moscow exported to the corners of its empire could trigger intervention from Moscow itself. And Serbia has set the precedent, even if the circumstances are far from identical.

There is also the specific threat of Muslim fundamentalism. At this point Europe's external and internal security interests converge. Whether Muslim fundamentalism is on the rise in North Africa or on the wane in Iran, Europeans are still among its prime targets, both within Europe's borders and without. Moreover, perceived persecution of Muslims anywhere can prompt co-extremists to spark unrest in Europe itself.

The end of the Cold War has not ushered in the end of arms proliferation, either conventional or nuclear. In fact, it has made it altogether more dangerous, for the superpowers' swords have yet to be converted successfully into ploughshares, and the makers and peddlers of weapons everywhere are turning their eyes to new, less easily identifiable clients. The control of the arms trade will be high on Europe's list of security interests, and the EU could mobilize Europe's considerable economic weight to achieve such control. The Union increasingly uses trade and aid agreements as levers to improve human rights and respect for democracy. For example, the Union now makes its trade agreements conditional on respect for human rights as a matter of course. It is also renegotiating the Lomé Convention, Europe's aid package for Africa, the Caribbean and the Pacific, with stronger conditions on democracy and human rights. It could go one step further, extracting in such circumstances commitments on arms control, as well as human rights.

How do we acquire one?

The need for such a policy is greater than ever. But the Maastricht Treaty provides the barest of skeletons which will need considerable fleshing out before the continent can react forcefully with any degree of unity to the world's trouble spots. Were it anything more, it could be counterproductive, attempting to straitjacket EU governments into common decisions for which Europe's varied and colourful history has not prepared them. But it does at least give Europe a foundation on which to build. The Treaty lays down five general objectives for a common European foreign and security policy. They are:

- To safeguard common values, fundamental interests and the independence of the Union.
- To strengthen the security of the Union and its member states in all ways.
- To preserve peace and strengthen international security, in accordance with the principles of the United Nations Charter* as well as the principles of the Helsinki Final Act† and the objectives of the Paris Charter.‡
- To promote international cooperation.
- To develop and consolidate democracy and the rule of law, and respect for human rights and fundamental freedom.

This is all very laudable, but what on earth does it mean in practice? Will it oblige young Danes to serve alongside

---

* The UN Charter signed at San Francisco in 1945 establishes a multilateral collective security system which has 'primary responsibility for the maintenance of international peace and security'. These objectives are exercised through the peaceful settlement of disputes between nations and the taking of enforcement action if required.

† The Helsinki Final Act (1975) concluded the first Conference on security and cooperation in Europe between the USSR, Eastern Europe and the West. The Act established three areas of cooperation for the CSCE states: political; economic and scientific; and humanitarian issues.

‡ *The Paris Charter* – The Charter of Paris for a New Europe was signed by the heads of all CSCE countries in the Paris Summit of November 1990. It provides for a new structure of relationships between the West and the former Soviet bloc. It also established the conflict prevention centre, which will serve to increase military transparency, and the office of free elections which will promote democracy.

French troops under German command? Will it mean open-ing European embassies around the world in place of, or alongside, national ones? Does it mean Europe must send joint flotillas to escort its oil tankers through the straits of Hormuz if they are jeopardized by fighting there? Will it bring German troops into Belfast? Will it lead to a common army, a common navy and a common airforce capable of acting without American approval or involvement both within Europe and beyond? And would Yugoslavia have broken up so bloodily if such a policy had existed before?

This is pure crystal-ball-gazing, but it does illustrate the wealth of options available, their extreme sensitivity, and the immense hurdles of history and tradition that governments would have to overcome before achieving any of them. Underlying the seemingly imprecise lines of Maastricht lies considerable and deliberate caution, and justifiably so, for the full implications of shared foreign policy and defence are colossal.

The EU's foreign ministers have begun to build on the foundations, sensibly adding three criteria to help define a pecking order of common European concerns: if a crisis erupts close to the Union's borders, or in a part of the world where the Union has a specific stake, or threatens its security interests in other ways, alarm bells should begin to ring. This in itself may prove difficult: Spain cares about Latin America in the way that France looks to North and West Africa and Indo-China, and Britain to the Commonwealth. Would Germany consider war in West Africa of sufficient common European interest? Even when all of Europe can focus on one country, governments may still have conflicting objectives. Europe dithered over Yugoslavia partly because countries bore different historical allegiances to the various Balkan republics, and because they disagreed over whether to acceler-ate the break-up by recognizing those republics early, or to hold back in the hope of negotiating a peaceful separation and averting the bloodbath that eventually occurred.

The risk is that European nations will take too long to overcome these difficulties, handicapping Europe in its urgent need to reflect, and influence, the changing balance of power. They will only give real body to the vague objectives of Maastricht if they learn to decide on common action more quickly and effectively than they do at present. Through European Political Cooperation, they are admirably fast at condemning a military coup in Haiti or supporting free elections in Namibia, but they lack a decision-making structure that forces them to split their differences and respond swiftly and firmly.

The Maastricht Treaty provides the first building blocks of such a structure. For example, member states will no longer simply 'endeavour' to decide and act together on foreign policy; now they 'shall define and implement a common foreign and security policy'. 'Coordination' and 'the convergence of positions' must now give way to 'concerted and convergent action'. And rather than merely 'ensuring that common principles and objectives are gradually developed and defined', European governments are committed to 'coordinate their action in international organizations' and 'uphold the common position' in such fora. If not all EU countries have a seat in such an organization, those that do must take a line consistent with the EU's overall approach.

In the past a common position in the UN or in UNCTAD,* for example, has been difficult to achieve because the Community has not developed a world view. Significantly, the Maastricht Treaty pushes for 'the common values and fundamental interests and independence of the Union'.

---

* Common positions within the UN are obtained by the constant collaboration of the twelve EU ambassadors. Wherever possible the twelve aim to vote together on UN resolutions.

Europe has never tried to define its geopolitical interests before. Maastricht will encourage it to do so. Indeed, this has given rise to proactive moves to stabilize borders and protect the rights of minorities in Eastern Europe, as with the initiative proposed by French Prime Minister Edouard Balladur.* Nothing as proactive as this emerged under the old-style EPC.

The draftsmen of Maastricht had to confront the age-old dichotomy that runs like the Rubicon down all areas of European decision-making: should the twelve governments decide foreign and security matters unanimously, allowing action to run into the sand because one country chooses to block it? Or should they agree by majority, ensuring a swifter European response to a crisis but possibly overriding the vital national interest of one isolated member country? Experience shows that majority voting breeds efficiency: Europe's Single Market owes its very existence to the fact that governments crossed that Rubicon and abandoned their veto over market-building measures by signing the Single European Act in 1986. But it can also foster resentment, as governments feel robbed of their sovereign right to decide sensitive matters themselves. This is especially true of areas where they differ ideologically, as with the treatment of workers, and historically, as with foreign policy and defence.

The draftsmen wisely opted at Maastricht for unanimity on foreign and security policy. They also decided to keep them 'intergovernmental', meaning that governments could work up joint policies on their own initiative rather than leaving the European Commission the sole right which it has under

* The Balladur initiative for security and stability in Europe was launched in June 1993 by Prime Minister Edouard Balladur. The initiative is designed to set up a framework within which Central and Eastern countries could negotiate when problems over frontiers or minorities arose.

the Rome Treaty to initiate measures and send them to the ministers for final approval. In addition the Commission itself can bring forward matters for consideration on its own initiative or at the suggestion of a member state.

The Commission's role in foreign and security policy will initially be fairly small since governments will retain the right to exercise a veto and disagree both with each other and with the Commission. Europe's more integrationist politicians may deplore governments' continuing hold over foreign policy and security but it is wholly unrealistic to believe that governments would allow themselves to be outvoted on such sensitive aspects as the dispatch of troops or the imposition of embargoes. Whether they ever will remains to be seen, but they are clearly not prepared to agree to this for the foreseeable future.

Another innovation of Maastricht is the ability conferred on the member states to define common 'action' as well as 'priorities'. Besides the involvement of the Commission and the stronger commitment to devise a common European position on issues, the Treaty also provides for decisions to be taken on 'common action'. Moreover, once member states have agreed unanimously on a course of action, they can decide how to put it into practice by a majority vote. This could involve anything from the use of diplomatic efforts to defuse a conflict, through to the imposition and monitoring of sanctions. But there is the further limitation that it will require a unanimous vote to decide that a particular issue is only a question of implementation which can be decided by majority vote.

Clearly Maastricht will not change Europe overnight. Does this mean that Europe will continue to disappoint the 'something must be done' advocates who call for urgent action to save Bosnians from slaughter? For Yugoslavia the answer is probably yes, for Europe is still, even post-Maastricht, not in a position to take military action on its own even if it wanted to. But what of future conflicts? The answer to this is also frustrating: Europe must build from the bottom upwards, whittling down its differences day by day rather than squeezing them into an ill-fitting structure of majority voting. This will not salvage Europe's battered image overnight. I remember a band of protesters bearing 'Save Bosnia' banners and heckling Europe's foreign ministers as they met in Luxembourg in autumn 1993: all they were chanting was 'Blah, blah, blah'. However unfortunate this is, Europe rightly needs to do a lot more talking and rehearsing before it could ever go to war with the unity, efficiency and readiness for sacrifice that war requires.

Let us suppose, for example, that war erupts in a hitherto peaceful state in the Middle East. Its population has a large immigrant community living in France. The country is not a major exporter of oil, so is of little strategic interest to the United States, although if the war spread it could provoke a wider conflagration which would surely affect the US. But it controls key shipping routes used by British merchant vessels exporting produce to the Far East. It is also host to major German and Dutch mining interests. Human rights are systematically being abused on a massive scale. Through the United Nations action could be taken in the form of political condemnation and sanctions, but if there is no response, what can Europe do alone?

At the moment, there is precious little Europe as such could do that would be taken seriously by a determined aggressor, beyond imposing political and economic isolation. Europe can and already does play a part in peace-keeping, though usually under UN auspices. Under Maastricht it could theoretically do so itself. The Treaty after all recognizes that the WEU should eventually become Europe's own coherent defence arm. But an independent defence cannot be invented overnight. Europe needs more than the theoretical provisions set down in Maastricht before it can develop the decisiveness and muscle required to exercise a military peace-making role.

The first serious steps towards European defence independence were taken at NATO summits in London, Rome and Brussels between 1990 and early 1994, with each successive summit endorsing further moves towards an independent military capability for Europe. By the time NATO leaders met in Brussels in January 1994, they were able to welcome a 'European Security and Defence Identity gradually emerging as the expression of a mature Europe' and to recognize that 'the emergence of a European Security and Defence Identity will strengthen the European pillar of the Alliance while reinforcing the Transatlantic link and will enable European allies to take greater responsibility for their common security and defence'.

But it has not been a simple journey. Ever since President Kennedy first floated the idea of a European pillar within NATO, it has foundered on the key question: how could Europe act without breaking the crucial transatlantic link on which Europe's security depends? Opinions have been sharply divided between those who wanted Europe to build up its own security structure within NATO, but with NATO keeping a firm clasp on all the puppet-strings; and those who wanted Europe's security to evolve into a separate and autonomous body, capable of acting on its own initiative. It was as though some saw the WEU as a siamese twin, while to others it had to be a good-natured child growing up to defend itself while staying loyal to its parents. I have always strongly favoured the latter.

So how have NATO leaders managed to reconcile these two views? They have in fact adopted the most logical solution, simply building on current practice. Under NATO rules, each country assigns forces to the alliance, but can withdraw them temporarily and use them for its own purposes under arrangements known as 'double hatting'. This happened most notably in the Gulf, where troops assigned to NATO took part in an engagement outside the NATO area together with their colleagues from other NATO countries but under national auspices. Troops assigned to UN duty are also usually participating under such arrangements, as have the British and Canadians in former Yugoslavia, for example. The Brussels NATO summit called for the development of 'separable but not separate capabilities which could respond to European requirements and contribute to Alliance security'. In other words, as Europe develops a coherent approach over time to its security through the WEU, if it assigns its troops, tanks, aircraft and other military handware *en bloc* to NATO it will also still be able to run its own independent operations.

Of course there are still many practical problems to overcome but the validity of a European defence objective has been accepted. In the process the differing objections and suspicions of France, Britain and the US, who together prevented the European pillar from developing during the Cold War, have been overcome.

The key change has been American readiness to accept that NATO material and logistics may be used for WEU operations, not just by the European wing of NATO. This is an absolutely crucial development because it means that creating a European defence capacity that is severable from NATO no longer involves the huge expense and complexity of building a separate logistic structure afresh. In fact, France's acceptance of a new arrangement is less of a surprise than it might at first appear. For it has gradually been realigning itself with NATO in recent years: its Chief of Staff joins his NATO colleagues in advising NATO ministers through the alliance's military committee, and French troops train alongside those of other NATO countries.

The French have traditionally been deeply suspicious of America's domination of European defence, refusing to forfeit altogether their right to fight independently, either with conventional or nuclear forces, should NATO be called to arms. But in agreeing to a European pillar of the alliance, France has swallowed its objections and in practice, if not in theory, accepted NATO's existing military command structure, no doubt feeling comfortable in doing so because of the 'separable' European capabilities which are envisaged.

The British too seem to have overcome their entrenched objections in agreeing to the quiet revolution which is taking place within NATO. They have in the past vigorously opposed any separate European defence which could act autonomously from NATO. They believed that a European defence would at best duplicate and at worst undermine the alliance, puncturing the effectiveness of NATO's existing command structure. Their objections have to a large extent been overcome by the modifications introduced into the WEU to enable it to work within NATO – putting its forces under the control of the Supreme Allied Commander where necessary but also giving it access to alliance assets for independent WEU operations. The British no doubt still harbour doubts about how this will work in practice, but they do appear to have accepted the principle that it may be necessary for British forces to serve alongside French, German and other troops in an autonomous European force and that, rather than enouraging US disengagement from Europe, this might actually help to strengthen the alliance. The trilateral meeting of French, German and British defence ministers in London at the end of January 1994, which would have been unthinkable a year or so earlier, is an indication of how much has changed.

Equally, the US is learning. In the past it has reacted to the prospect of an independent European defence in much the same way as a father behaves towards a rebellious teenager: happy to loosen the grip on its increasingly expensive and burdensome offspring, but too accustomed to forty years of unchallenged leadership to do so lightly. It seems ready to get used to the fact that, though a less tidy option at first sight, an autonomous European defence within NATO will be able to perform some functions better than NATO itself.

Russia, for example, is gradually adopting a constructive approach to NATO, but this may take some years to mature; that twilight period is precisely the time when instability in Eastern Europe is most likely to erupt. But if NATO were to spread further eastwards, it could stir a few ghosts from the past, compelling Russia to react vigorously, not least because some of Russia's most fractious and rebellious neighbours – Armenia, Ajerbaijan, Georgia, the Baltics, even Ukraine – would then fall worryingly close to NATO's sphere of influence. NATO's 'Partnership for Peace' with the Central and Eastern European countries launched in January 1994 attempts to walk this dangerous tightrope between stabilizing Central and Eastern Europe and bowing to the growls of the Russian bear. Here the development of a European defence will play a critical part in desensitizing the issue for Russia. If the WEU really does develop into Europe's security arm then membership of the Union, which is the declared ambition of the East Europeans, will automatically mean membership of the WEU and then no doubt of NATO as well. The advance of Western security into the East will then no longer be a threat from an old adversary but rather an organic part of the reunification of Europe.

The next step will be to make the European defence identity work. In the first instance we will need to give teeth to the WEU itself. Conceived in 1948 by Europe's wartime allies – Britain, France, Holland, Belgium and Luxembourg – the WEU took in Germany and Italy six years later, after

NATO was created and Europe's first attempt at a fully fledged defence policy – the European Defence Community – collapsed. Despite successive attempts to kiss it back to life, the WEU lay dormant like Sleeping Beauty until 1989. If the WEU now evolves into Europe's first independent defence structure, Maastricht may prove to have been Prince Charming. Before this happens, NATO and the WEU authorities will need to work closely together and will both need to make changes in their structures and procedures if the separable pillar is going to be operational.

Once these problems have been overcome the European pillar may in practice spring into life sooner than anticipated. For the WEU could benefit from a separate development on the European defence scene. Anxious to maintain the momentum of renewed interest in European defence, France and Germany agreed in 1990 to create a common territorial brigade under joint command, and Spain, Italy and Belgium swiftly showed interest in joining too. Based in Strasbourg, the 35,000-strong Eurocorps will become the seedling of a future joint European defence force. It has earned the blessing of NATO, falling under its command where defence of NATO territory is required as well as for peace-keeping, peace enforcement operations and humanitarian actions. It will remain of little military consequence for many years; but it could help test in practice the kind of theoretical military cooperation that the Western European Union is bound to propose in principle.

At first blush, this competing development may seem a recipe for disaster, but such institutional competition has often produced the most suitable model in the past: the European Union's own early competition with the Council of Europe can testify to this. Once the Eurocorps is more organised it will be able to slip into the European pillar framework which is being established in the Alliance. In the first instance, it will help manage crises and keep the peace outside NATO territory, under the auspices of the UN or CSCE. Over time it must develop the ability to take part in real peace enforcement as well.

Where does this leave the European Union on the world stage? The Union should channel its efforts into doing politically what it has performed so well economically: gradually dismantling Europe's historical barriers so that governments themselves will stand square whenever international crises erupt rather than bickering incessantly beneath a public veil of unity. It must then persuade governments to express their burgeoning consensus through more efficient decision-making procedures. Ultimately there is no reason why the WEU should not be merged with the European Union, which would simply have a military wing, within NATO, but capable of being detached from it and used for specifically European purposes. We are a long way from achieving such an objective, and it would be a mistake to seek to achieve it on any basis other than consensus, but if it *were* achieved it would enhance the effectiveness of the European Union's foreign policy and security role and be the logical conclusion of this aspect of the Union's development.

Conclusion

The direction of Europe's security has undoubtedly changed, but the destination is still far from clear. The proliferation of new peace structures and initiatives, while maybe harmless in itself, epitomizes the uncertainty gripping the continent. At least, we assure ourselves, Western Europe no longer suffers a direct threat to its own territory. That may be true, but it calls for a far more complex approach to foreign policy and defence than we have known for forty years, and at a time when recession and the elusive 'peace dividend' have driven high defence budgets out of fashion. Europe has to rethink the very shape of its security stance knowing it must grow its own military wing but unsure how to handle America in the process. Europe must take its time, not least because quick-remedy prescriptions have drifted out of fashion in Europe as its governments realize their historical differences are deeper than some Euro-enthusiasts would have had us believe. Clearly, Europe cannot assume foreign and security powers in isolation from the changing priorities of its old ally, America, and its new one, Russia.

So how should Europe proceed? The European Union does already have an embryonic policy on foreign and security affairs, but so far it produces words, not actions. Words do matter, and when coupled with the EU's economic muscle, they can produce powerfully dissuasive results. But the day when Europe takes joint, decisive and effective military action is a long way off. If Europe ever achieves such a potential, as I believe it can and should, it will only be after years of exhaustive dialogue to assess how Europe could respond better to specific crises united rather than alone; and it should rehearse those options thoroughly through Eurocorps, the Western European Union and other emerging models. The first sketch of a joint foreign and security policy is there, in the Maastricht Treaty, and the need to fill it in has never been greater, but rolling Europe's war-torn history into a single set of joint objectives with which to face a volatile world cannot be achieved overnight.

CHAPTER 8

Central and Eastern Europe and
the Former Soviet Union

Peace has never managed to take root for very long in Europe. The continent has been a shifting picture of conquests, whether Greek, Roman, Nordic, Ottoman, Austro-Hungarian or Napoleonic, all driven by greed and justified by king and country, or by religion. Like drops of oil on water, Europe's ancient tribes have shifted around the continent, expanding and buffeting their borders, the strong subsuming the weak only to break up later into smaller units which have gradually regrouped in harmony, as in Germany or Italy, or in hostility, as in much of the Balkans.

The Second World War seemed like more of the same, as one man's mendacious rhetoric persuaded a nation to push greedily outwards, clothing hegemony in the thin guise of order, anti-Semitism and anti-Communism. But somehow the ending was different. The old Europe no longer existed, for the continent itself had split in two, with one half convalescing under the strong but welcome protection of America, and the other half hived off into an alien, inhuman and radically un-European social and economic structure, where it lay incarcerated for over forty years.

Wolfgang Amadeus Mozart, the embodiment of European culture, shuttled busily between Vienna and Prague. History is awash with such examples of musicians, artists, politicians and famous travellers criss-crossing the continent in peace and war. Mozart would certainly recoil in horror at the unparalleled ferocity of the Second World War; but he would stare in even greater disbelief at the outcome. And yet to my generation, the divide seemed so utterly final that right up until 1989, Western Europe made its economic plans for the future with little thought for the East, while gearing its military planning almost exclusively to fending off the Communist threat. But the moment East Germany's 'allies' condoned the exodus of refugees who began heading West by the train-load, cracks appeared in the Iron Curtain, and it was torn down in no time. The changes which swept through the former Eastern bloc from 1989 onwards were all the more momentous for being so unexpected.

The task facing us is every bit as historically significant as the one facing Jean Monnet, Robert Schuman and Winston Churchill, who sought to heal the age-old rift between France and Germany as the foundation of a new peaceful order in Western Europe. Like the founders of the European Community, we must bridge the gap between East and West, building on post-Soviet freedom while preventing the ensuing vacuum from filling up with vicious ethnic or nationalistic feuds. In some ways our task will require an even greater leap of faith than the task that faced the founding fathers of post-war Western Europe: the East–West divide was frozen for so long that few of today's leaders and law-makers have much first-hand experience of Europe as a single continent.

Those states which have emerged from the Soviet empire clearly face the biggest changes of all, making the West's problems look small by comparison. But the West too, particularly the European Union, is slowly waking to the need to adopt new attitudes. The EU is realizing that minor alterations will not suffice, for the very structure of the European house has changed. The states of Central and Eastern Europe are not just friendly, impoverished neighbours, to be palmed off with aid, trade and patronage. They are quite simply members of the same family. At different stages they will gradually become firmly rooted democracies, sharing similar values, exploiting the same markets and requiring the same security as their co-European partners to the west.

Some will eventually join the European Union, if and when they are willing and able to do so. This will present Western Europe with perhaps its greatest challenge of all. Just a few years ago they all shared the overriding goal of throwing off the yoke of Communism and Soviet domination; since 1989, their differences have floated back to the surface as they rediscover their national identities, as well as reshape their economies to fit a tougher, less artificial industrial and commercial world. Yet there is a common objective shared by all Central and Eastern European nations, despite the ethnic tensions which exist and their struggles to compete economically: their prime target is to return to the European fold. For Russia even that political certainty is missing, for it has lost an empire and needs to redefine its role in a more uncertain world. And the former republics of the USSR, while mostly nominally united through the Commonwealth of Independent States, are casting around for alternative alliances in Europe and Central Asia, falteringly restoring their old economic ties with Russia while in some cases fighting hideously between themselves.

The European Union must tailor its approach to the specific needs and aspirations of each and every one of the emerging states to its east, without assuming from their recent history that those needs are identical. None the less, there will be one particular feature which will distinguish our future ties with them: whether we and they share accession to the Union as a policy objective. At their Copenhagen Summit in June 1993, Union leaders explicitly recognized Poland, Hungary, the Czech Republic, Slovakia, Bulgaria and Romania as prospective EU members. These nations, together with the Baltics, Albania, Slovenia and the other former Yugoslav states, have to be regarded in a different light from Russia and the CIS republics.

Central and Eastern Europe and the Baltic states

Beneath the public enthusiasm for the reunification of Europe, many in the West privately recoil in fear at the prospect of Eastern states actually joining the European Union. It is odd that they should be considered part of the same European history but should not share a common future. Some fear for those countries themselves, arguing that membership would shake their fragile economies and democracies apart as they are forced to shed forty years of stagnation and totalitarianism too quickly. Others fear for the impact on the Union itself, whose decision-making abilities would grind to a halt as it sought to satisfy too many more voices. Yet in 1986, Spain and Portugal emerged impoverished from decades of dictatorship and partial economic isolation to join the EU. Their progress ever since has dispelled those fears: they have consolidated their own democracies, boosted economic growth and even accelerated joint European decisions in many cases, notably in areas of Single Market legislation. Greece, though flagging economically, has buried the dictatorship of the Colonels for good. Finally there are those who fear that by enlarging eastwards into Central and Eastern Europe, as well as northwards into Scandinavia, the Union will absorb more liberal-minded countries, diluting the will of its current members to retain trade barriers and defend Europe's beleaguered industry from world competition. But to resist membership because of a country's liberal complexion would be dangerous folly, and go completely against the grain of the Union's current trend of development.

The Baltics have their eyes firmly on Union membership. They are close geographically and commercially, and in

Estonia's case linguistically, to Scandinavia. Estonia already trades freely with Finland, and wants similar treatment from the EU, ahead of Latvia and Lithuania, which are less economically advanced. Unlike most of the USSR, the Baltic states were independent between the two world wars, so EU membership would hardly mean casting off the moorings of history. They are small in size and population, so would not cause the EU ship to capsize. Soviet domination has left its scars on the economy and the people; of all the former Soviet satellites it is here that ethnic Russians are most prominent yet feel most threatened, making EU membership altogether trickier than might otherwise be the case. None the less the case for ultimate membership of the Union is a very powerful one, which should not be resisted.

The European Union is not an empire, but a voluntary meeting of states. The desire to join must come from the will of the Eastern European peoples themselves, as must the success of their economic and social reforms. They cannot and will not be forced in, but neither must they be excluded. Indeed it should be repeatedly made clear that those who want to join the Union will be welcomed. The aid which is currently given to them is designed to prepare them for accession in due course if they continue to be of the view they want to join us. Union governments have committed themselves to accepting any European state that is ready and willing to join.* The Union can and must help, not just for historic or altruistic motives but through enlightened self-

---

* Membership of the Community by other European countries was envisaged as early as the Treaty of Rome, which calls upon 'the other peoples of Europe who share their ideal to join in their efforts . . .' EC heads of state sent an even stronger signal specifically to the East by declaring, at their Copenhagen Summit in June 1993, that 'the associated countries in Central and Eastern Europe that so desire shall become members of the European Union'.

interest too. Failure could bring economic instability and social unrest, provoking mass immigration; success will enhance the security of Europe, create a bigger market for our industry, but above all enable Europe to face the world as a broadly united continent rather than as a privileged section of that historic and geographic entity.

THE ECONOMY

The first step to achieve this goal must be the rebuilding of the economies of Eastern and Central Europe.

The first words of Romanian that I learned, without making any effort, were '*economia de piazza*', meaning 'market economy'. The language of the market is echoed across the East with vigour and zeal, not as one side of a sterile academic debate about free trade, but as the emblem of future prosperity. Yet how does a country set about building a market economy out of the ruins of a command system deprived of business incentive and run from Moscow? The initial impact of market forces has sometimes seemed one of devastation. Poland and Slovakia have been forced to slash jobs in their steel industries, for their old Soviet market no longer exists. As I saw vividly when visiting the European Union's land reform programme near Plovdiv, Bulgaria, you cannot even begin to boost agricultural efficiency until farmland is put back into private hands. And when that happens the farm machinery is Brobdingnagian in its unsuitability for the small family farms that are replacing collectivization.

Nothing on this scale has been tried before, and the search for one model to apply to all countries is fruitless. Eyes turn to German reunification as the only existing example, but it is a misleading precedent for others: the former GDR has been absorbed lock, stock and barrel into a unified Germany, entailing the immediate abolition of its currency, considerable funds from the federal treasury, and instant EC membership. That is a situation which is quite different from the one obtaining elsewhere in Central and Eastern Europe.

Eastern European countries need greater access to Western markets to sell more goods, and more Western expertise to streamline their industries to produce those goods better, faster and more cheaply. They also need further aid to improve transport and communications, and to build a sound, lean administration to stop economic reform sinking into a quagmire of bureaucracy. That way they will catch up gradually, and at their own varying speeds, with their Western partners.

The European Union, through the PHARE programme,* pays some 1 billion ecu a year towards projects as diverse as reopening the Budapest Stock Exchange, promoting exports through the Chambers of Commerce in Warsaw and Gdansk, upgrading orphanages in Romania, safeguarding against accidents at nuclear installations in Bulgaria, building a network of small companies in Slovakia, and helping all of the above to sell off state-run industries from the Communist era. In all projects, the goal is the same: to help the East cut its own path to long-term prosperity.

As the region develops, so its needs are growing more sophisticated. At the outset, food, spare parts and other emergency provisions were top priority, just to keep the system from collapsing. Now its entire macro- and micro-economic framework must change, for example by introducing a new banking and financial system and new accountancy, taxation and bankruptcy laws. The Union's aid programme has encountered teething problems, and must adapt too. More decisions

---

* Eleven countries are currently eligible for aid under PHARE: Albania, Bulgaria, the Czech Republic, Slovakia, Estonia, Hungary, Latvia, Lithuania, Poland, Romania and Slovenia. There is a proposal to include the former Yugoslav Republic of Macedonia too.

need farming out to the regions and governments which will feel the effects of the reform projects, to ensure that decisions are taken by those who know the situation on the ground. In 1990, the beneficiary countries urgently needed 'technical assistance' – Western aid and expertise to help them build up the fabric of a modern market economy after decades of Communist mismanagement. Over time this has been overtaken by the growing need for support to encourage investment in transport, telecommunications and other infrastructure, as well as in companies and farms. The PHARE programme is changing in step with the countries it seeks to help. At their Copenhagen Summit, EC leaders decided that up to 15 per cent of PHARE funds could go to aid investment in infrastructure.

However, it is trade, at least as much as aid, that is uppermost in the minds of managers and ministers in Prague, Warsaw, Sofia and Budapest. But when it comes to lifting trade barriers, as with EU membership itself, the West does not always match the zeal of the East. That is because people allow the perceived short-term threat to cloud their view of the long-term, and in some cases even immediate, gains. The EU is by far the biggest trading partner for Central and Eastern Europe. Between 1989 and 1992, the exports of the six associated countries to the EU grew by 87 per cent, up from 11.6 billion ecu to 21.7 billion ecu. And yet over the same period, the EU's trade deficit of 577 billion ecu with these countries turned into a surplus of 2.8 billion ecu. Freer trade with the East is, therefore, in our interest. And while Central and Eastern Europe buys and sells over half of its trade with the EU, the latter depends for just 3 per cent of its trade with them.

EU heads of state decided in Copenhagen in June 1993 to speed up the timetable for the complete removal of tariffs and other trade barriers against Eastern imports. As a result, the

EU's commitment to open its doors fully to trade from the associated countries within five years has been accelerated to removing all barriers to trade in industrial goods in three years, except where this would have a serious impact on the EU's own sensitive industries. The Union's so-called 'Europe Agreements' with Poland, Hungary, Slovakia, the Czech Republic, Bulgaria and Romania already foresaw free trade as an indispensable training ground for eventual membership; the decision to usher it in two years earlier for most products should bolster the resolve of the people of Eastern Europe, many of whom currently see market reform as little but suffering and sacrifice.

Western industry's fears are not, however, altogether without foundation. In the current recession, some industries are so sensitive to even small increases in cut-price imports that they need temporary protection. For those sectors of the economy where the Union itself operates a significantly interventionist policy, such as steel, it is necessary to bring the countries of Eastern and Central Europe into the thinking when planning future policies long before they actually become members of the Union. If, for example, the Union encouraged a restructuring of the steel industry, it should draw the Eastern and Central European steel companies into the equation when planning and implementing its policy. Doing this will not be easy but it is the only alternative to continuing friction or the resentment caused by severe limitations on the access granted to the EU market.

Sometimes competition can turn unfair. There is a grave risk of the East swamping the West with certain commodities, either dumped deliberately by manufacturers to make up for the loss of their customers in Russia, or flooding in cheaply from companies where prices are artificially low because they continue to be supported by the state. The Union has a series of trade defence instruments, notably its anti-dumping, anti-subsidy and safeguard rules, to ward off that danger. These are vital, but they are defensive, and therefore second-best in my mind. Western Europe needs to go on the offensive, pressing its Eastern partners to apply the same rules of conduct as we do if they are to exploit our markets. The six aspiring EU members have undertaken to apply European Community competition rules to their own companies three years after their Europe Agreements enter into force. If this works, it will curb the Communist legacy of runaway state subsidies, as well as preventing governments from paying company overheads, such as energy and pollution costs, normally borne by the manufacturer in market economies. Europe East and West should harbour no illusions: creating a level playing field in the Union will seem like child's play when compared to doing so in Central and Eastern Europe. But it needs to be done if trade is really to flow freely without continued suspicions that goods from the East are coming in unfairly.

Admitting a significant number of new countries would inevitably put an intolerable strain on the current machinery of the Union. The right answer to this problem is not to refuse membership, but rather to make the necessary changes in the institutional machinery, so that admitting new countries does not clog up the works and make it difficult for decisions to be taken and implemented efficiently.

Any attempt to force the pace of EU membership, however, would have dire side-effects, and I believe neither in fixed target dates nor artificial waiting lists. The rules governing Western Europe's Single Market would at present be an intolerable burden even for the Polish, Czech or Hungarian economies, already several steps ahead of the others. The EU is essentially a bargain between governments which agree to open their borders to each other, on condition that in return tough common rules are observed on anything from food labelling to worker safety and pollution control. Until such time as those rules would help, not hinder, economic development in the East, EU membership is out of the question. That moment will be highly unpredictable, and will certainly vary from country to country, so I see no reason why we should wait to admit them *en bloc*. For each one, entry negotiations must begin once they are ready, able and willing to join. How this can be done will be discussed in Chapter 9.

Ethnic tensions apart, the biggest casualty of the post-Communist era has been the collapse of trade between former Soviet allies. From 1945 onwards, Moscow assiduously twisted the economies of its East European satellites to suit its military and political objectives, creating an artificial web of economic interdependence through the COMECON trading system, forcing them to divert their sales away from natural trading partners in Western Europe and towards Russia itself. (The sheer folly of Soviet economic policy is best illustrated by the drainage of the Aral Sea between Kazakhstan and Uzbekistan, an ecological disaster in itself, in order to grow cotton.) This system disintegrated as Eastern Europe lunged for political freedom, misreading the encouragement and jubilation in the West as a sign that it would instantly fulfil their economic needs. Economic reality, it seems, was trampled under foot in the stampede to escape Communism.

The European Union must help its Eastern partners to relay the trading tracks between themselves, where this makes economic sense, while laying new ones across the continent from east to west. This cannot be a substitute for EU membership, but a vital complement to it, as well as making sound economic sense. There are no warm-up clubs or waiting rooms prior to EU membership, nor must there ever be. Not even the European Free Trade Association (EFTA), grouping most of Western Europe outside the Union, fits that description: Britain and Portugal were in EFTA before joining the Union, but Ireland, Greece and Spain were not; and Switzerland has opted not to join the vast Single Market being created between EFTA and the Union.*

Inter-regional trade is every bit as vital for the East as for Western Europe. Under Moscow's central planning the East Europeans were forced to neglect trade even between themselves and prevented from trading with their former partners in the West. And yet this, sadly, may have blinkered their view, as their eyes swivel sharply from East to West without settling on each other. Yes, Poland, Hungary, Slovakia and the Czech Republic have formed the 'Visegrad' group ostensibly to promote inter-regional trade; but there is a risk they will treat it more as an antechamber to EU membership than as a workshop for chiselling away the differences between their own market rules. It is Brussels' job to offer support while persuading them persistently that the latter will help lead them through to the former.

SOCIOPOLITICAL ASPECTS

Ditching one ideology for another overnight is proving an extremely painful business. The peoples of Eastern Europe have knuckled under, stoically accepting high inflation, falling living standards and the removal of an elaborate social safety net, provoking mass unemployment and, in some cases, poverty. Thankfully, there is a glimmer of light at the end of the tunnel: new cars are emerging from FIAT production lines in Poland and other consumer goods are burgeoning. Public patience is beginning to wear thin, nevertheless, and public readiness to suffer the short-term costs will increasingly speed

---

* Originally a British-inspired body created to counterbalance the influence of the Community itself, EFTA soon grouped most of Western Europe outside the Community into a single free trade area. It has now spawned the European Economic Area, which spreads the benefits of the EU's internal market throughout almost all of Western Europe as of the beginning of 1994.

up or slow down reform. The dilemma now facing new political parties is whether to take unpopular decisions quickly or to phase them in gradually, lessening the impact by spreading them over time. Unfortunately, democracy itself is new, spawning political parties and coalitions which lack the organization to agree on painful but vital policies, and the stomach to stick to them.

What can Western Europe do? There are two ways it can help, and two ways it can harm the resolve of Eastern Europe to hold to the reforms it has launched. To help, it must first offer the genuine prospect of access to its markets. Eastern Europe's enthusiasm for the Union's promise to lift all trade barriers within five years has been minimized by distrust: many believe we will retain barriers against the products they produce best, such as beef, textiles, steel and other commodities, by invoking anti-dumping or other trade weapons at the drop of a hat; in the spring of 1993 they attacked the Community's ban on beef imports as naked protectionism, despite evidence that foot-and-mouth disease had entered the Community from Eastern Europe. To avoid unnecessary loss of trust, the EU must use its trade defence armoury sparingly, for as short a period as is strictly necessary, taking care to explain its motives and to seek ways of settling trade disputes 'out of court'.

Secondly, the Union can help in the very reform of social security itself. Eastern governments can no longer afford the generous healthcare, childcare, training and leisure facilities of the past which were often provided by paternalistic and inherently loss-making state-owned enterprises. In Poland, PHARE is financing a programme to train general practitioners and health managers, while in the Czech Republic it is helping to computerize the social security system.

The Union must avoid two traps over the next decade. The first is indifference: if the East continues to suspect the Union of foot-dragging on its commitment to eventual free trade, and the EU does little to dispel that suspicion, the people of Eastern Europe will lose faith, and their own reforms will drag. The second snare is paternalism: the local population ultimately knows better than Western experts what it needs and what will work. Moreover, affluent Europe is far from a shining example of social well-being: we have not rid our society of exclusion and discrimination, and unemployment remains the biggest sore on our economy. PHARE and all other Western aid programmes must be driven more and more by the demands of the local beneficiaries.

The West can also foster the construction of democracy itself. Through the PHARE Democracy Programme, the Union offers 'marriage broking' between non-governmental bodies from both sides of the continent. It has been helping Albania and Romania to train lawyers, prison officers and policemen, in order to develop fair and humane systems for trying, sentencing and incarcerating offenders; the International Federation of Journalists is helping develop an independent local press in Poland; and Public Services International, a world umbrella group for public sector trade unions, is helping to nurture such unions in the Baltics.

ETHNIC TENSIONS

Since the Second World War, the European Community has successfully created a climate in which it is inconceivable that the existence of national minorities within member states could lead to territorial disputes. Yet in Eastern Europe, just the opposite has occurred: long-standing ethnic tension was bottled up by Soviet hegemony, and is now spilling out with a vengeance. As the tragedy of Bosnia shows, forcibly combining nationality with territory can lead to disaster. Does Western Europe's responsibility for the East mean it should intervene in ethnic and other disputes, and is it equipped to do so?

Whether or not it can or should do more, the Union can at least act as mediator, as it has done successfully in the long-running dispute between Hungary and Slovakia over the Gabcikovo–Nagymaros dam. Plans have existed since the 1950s to build a series of locks on the Danube to improve shipping, flood control and for electricity production. Hungary and Czechoslovakia signed a Treaty providing for a dam to be built at Gabcikovo in Slovakia, and Nagymaros in Hungary. Environmental opposition grew in Hungary in 1989 to 1990, and the Hungarians decided to halt construction on their side while opposing the Czechoslovaks' decision to push ahead. In 1992 both sides asked the European Commission to mediate, and it has since successfully urged them to submit their grievances to the International Court of Justice in the Hague rather than fighting it out between themselves. As well as helping on the ground, therefore, the European Union's example of burying old enmities through voluntary, gradual integration will undoubtedly catch on in the East.

Meanwhile, events in former Yugoslavia have shown all too clearly and tragically that for the moment the possibility of ethnic conflict breaking out into violence is all too present. The unpalatable truth is that none of the countries in the Union has actually been prepared to contemplate military intervention on the scale needed to stop the conflict, and there can be no guarantee that there would be a different response if a similar situation were to arise elsewhere.

The only realistic hope must be that the Union might be able to intervene at a certain stage with 'softer' alternatives designed to nip conflict in the bud. Mediation is one such alternative. Economic and political sanctions are another. The tight belt of sanctions around Serbia and Montenegro, agreed and monitored by the Community, has not stopped the war, far from it; but it has brought Serbia's economy to its knees, and the Belgrade government plus its Bosnian and Croatian co-belligerents to the negotiating table. This may seem a hollow success, but it is also reasonable to believe that sanctions have prevented the conflict spilling over into neighbouring areas. A system for handling ethnic and border disputes under the European Union at an early stage, along the lines proposed by the French Prime Minister, Edouard Balladur, is now being actively considered.

CONCLUSION

The countries of Western and Eastern Europe have a common future as well as a common past. Future EU membership will offer the best guarantee of political stability and economic prosperity. And the very prospect of that day eventually arriving offers the best bulwark against the danger of an angry electorate beating moderate politicians off the path of painful economic reform. The Union must hold to its promise of open markets, and avoid the pitfalls of protectionism. It must look beyond its own job queues and other recessionary troubles and lay the groundwork now for one market tomorrow. It would be short-sighted for the West to assume change should happen only in the East. If the Union fails to adapt its own industries and institutions to the requirements of a fully reunified Europe, it risks being tarred by the same brush as the old Communists themselves, who blithely refused to notice as their world slipped away from beneath their feet.

Former Soviet Union

RUSSIA

Successive failed attempts by Europeans to conquer Russia, and Moscow's own forty-year domination of half the European continent, should by now have taught both sparring partners a clear lesson: any bid by one to control the other will end in disaster for both sides. History also shows that Europe and Russia each considers the other to be of primordial importance to its security. Hitler marched on Russia in 1941 in order, ostensibly, to fight off the encroaching threat of Communism; Stalin fought back to defend the Bolshevik revolution from the spread of Fascism. Hitler went practically to the gates of Moscow, while Stalin drove him right back to Berlin; for both, 'defence' entailed the near-annihilation of the other. When Stalin arrived in Berlin, the threat of Fascism evolved seamlessly into the menace of Capitalism, and so there he stayed, 'defending' Russia against Europe and Europe against America. The moral of history since the day Napoleon was beaten back by the Russian winter can only be that when two giants live so close, they must learn to get on like good neighbours.

Since the Russian empire imploded, it has become abundantly clear to Europe that a weak Russia affects its security just as much as a strong one. Europe views Russia as though it were a form of potential energy, a latent force which will be channelled eventually into either malevolence or benevolence, but a force which will never dissolve. With Central and Eastern Europe, the European Union knows deep down that it shares the same destiny, although its governments may disagree on the means to achieve that; but with Russia, it is unsure both of the road and the destination. Europe has yet to work out with any long-term vision how it should respond to change in Russia. Instead, it reacts to events as they dramatically unfold one by one. It is a policy vacuum which urgently needs to be filled.

I first became aware of this vacuum at a meeting of European foreign ministers in Luxembourg on 4 April 1993. Presidents Clinton and Yeltsin had met in Vancouver the day before to agree a massive package of American aid for

Russia. The US was bandying vast sums of money about with little evident intention of providing it all, indeed much was to come from other Western donors. But Washington was happy to take the credit. Meanwhile, back in Luxembourg, the ministers were to discuss increasing the scope for the Community's trade with Russia in order to encourage economic and political reform there. Instead of capitalizing on the Yeltsin/Clinton summit to make their own political declaration, the ministers merely stuck to the scripts provided by their officials, missing the chance to achieve a breakthrough in an issue which dominated the global agenda for the rest of the year. Fortunately this attitude changed, and contacts with Moscow accelerated in the run-up to President Yeltsin's visit to Brussels in December 1993.

Through its earlier unwillingness, indeed its inability, to focus on questions of such magnitude, Europe allowed the United States to take the lead, even though its trade with Russia dwarfs that of America. Even now, Europe's political profile with Russia is not commensurate with its economic importance. We still have some way to go to define the nature of the relationship we want. I do not see Russia as a future member of the European Union, nor do I believe Russia wishes to join, but that should not prevent us developing a coherent, close political relationship, matching the importance of our economic ties.

Politics will drive the EU's future relationship with Russia, and the EU's desire to help Russia is clearly founded on the continuation of the Russian reform process, which is bound to be a highly uncertain factor. But we must do everything we can to sustain that process, and our economic relationship is the key. The EU is Russia's primary trading partner. According to the OECD in 1992, the Union imported over twenty times more from the former USSR in terms of value than did North America, and eight times more than did

Japan. Eighty per cent of these imports came from Russia itself. This left the Community with a trade deficit of 2.75 billion ecu, while North America ran a 3 billion ecu trade surplus. Furthermore, Russia could become a major supplier of energy and raw materials, with European companies helping exploit its rich resources, and trade can only increase if market reforms take root and Russian purchasing power grows. We simply buy and sell too much with the Russians to allow our relationship to drift onwards unguided.

It is far too early, however, to open each other's doors fully to each other's business. In an open market with Europe, Russia would lose outright. When it comes to import barriers, the Union has already set the bar far lower than Russia: our average tariff on Russian imports is 1.1 per cent and falling, while Russia still protects its market with average tariffs of 15 per cent. Free trade now would blast across Russia's fragile companies like a cold wind from the steppes. Europe, however, is offering Russia the *prospect* of free trade at some stage in the future, though with no specific deadline. In 1998, both sides will meet to see if the conditions are right to start negotiations.

Russian industry is gripped by a far more immediate crisis, relegating the idea of unfettered trade to a distant dream. Its factories continue to churn out goods for markets which no longer exist, notably in defence, and as they cast around for new buyers, Europe's industry feels the strain. Take aluminium, for example. The Union's imports of Russian aluminium have risen twenty-three-fold in three years, from 15,000 tonnes in 1990 to 350,000 tonnes in 1992, and prices have slumped from 1,336 ecu to 917 ecu a tonne, well below prices on the London Metal Exchange. If Russian industry was merely over-producing, it could prescribe itself a clean if painful remedy by closing factories and cutting capacity drastically, but the illness is more complex, and the cure more elusive: the military market has vanished, and there are as yet few civilian customers to replace it. Cut-price exporting seems like an easy way of tiding industry over, and it works, but with serious side-effects: ironically the Communist legacy – high subsidies, low energy costs and the near-absence of other overheads – makes Russian industry seem highly competitive, because prices are not related to real costs. This backfires elsewhere, notably in Europe, where aluminium manufacturers are also struggling with high unemployment as they, too, scour the globe for new customers.

Europe must help Russia tackle the problem at source, as well as defending its producers against unfair imports through the use of trade policy instruments. This means assisting Russian industry to modernize itself, so that it can develop its own market and compete fairly on the world market, without subsidized prices and without polluting the environment. Russia may be seen as a land of opportunity, but many would-be investors from the West still dare not take the plunge, seeing it as too precarious a place to do business. Russia must be helped and encouraged to provide effective protection for foreign investors' assets, guaranteeing them the right to export their profits. For if not, those investors will choose to build their factories and sink their oil drills elsewhere.

This is only one aspect of the massive transformation required to modernize Russian society in all respects. Creating democracy and a market economy in Russia is a far more formidable task than in Eastern and Central Europe, both because of its sheer size and diversity, and because it has lacked a historic memory of what democracy and a market economy could actually be like. None the less, despite some worrying political signals, Russia's present rulers say they are determined to continue to move in that direction, and it is in our interest as well as theirs to help them to do so.

The European Union has been deploying over half a billion ecu a year since 1991 to fund Western experts to help Russia and its former Soviet neighbours privatize their industries, repair and run their nuclear power stations safely, reorganize the ports of St Petersburg, Odessa and elsewhere, distribute food better, and modernize Russia's air traffic control, as well as encouraging Russian and European businesses to form joint ventures and invest in each other's countries. Administered through the EU's programme of technical assistance for the Commonwealth of Independent States, or TACIS, this funding may seem a drop in the ocean alongside the Herculean task of rebuilding Russian industry, but it is a start.

For Eastern Europe, the path ahead is fairly clear – they want to join the wider Europe, and ultimately the Union itself, as soon as possible. The Union's future relationship with Russia and its neighbours must necessarily be open-ended. We must help modernize Russian industry and open our markets gradually to its products, but without opening those markets fully until Russia's own free market reforms are irreversible and its trading practices in line with international rules. We must slim down the restrictions on Russian companies so that they are able to establish in Europe, but without creating free movement for Russian workers themselves; for while most Russians' first choice would be to earn a living at home, the current economic turmoil could drive some of Russia's vast population westwards, bursting at the seams Europe's capacity to absorb immigration.

DEALING WITH RUSSIA'S NEIGHBOURS

For all its ideological abhorrence of Soviet hegemony, Europe was forced to accept the USSR as one country, and it learned to deal with it as such. That habit is now proving fiendishly difficult to discard. Russia, for example, has several thousand miles of coastline, while Tadjikistan has no coast at all, yet when I took charge of the European Union's relations with the region in January 1993, I found that the European Commission had a mandate to negotiate identical fishing agreements with both. Clearly the provisions on trade and fish will be more relevant for Russia than Tadjikistan. Their varying histories, societies and aspirations demand that Europe differentiate diligently between them.

Ukraine, Belarus and Moldova understandably seem unsure of their future economic and political allegiances. Ukraine is Russia's main source of food and the main conduit for Russia's trade with the West. They are extremely dependent on one another for their economic welfare, so it is of key strategic importance to Europe that Moscow and Kiev should stay friends. That fact may militate against EU membership, but in favour of free trade as soon as it is feasible, together with the establishment of common rules to protect investments, as well as deeper dialogue on foreign policy and defence.

Europe cannot yet entertain long-term economic or political ties with the Caucasian republics – Georgia, Armenia and Azerbaijan – for relations with them are muddied by complex ethnic turmoil and territorial conflict. In the Central Asian Republics – Kazakhstan, Turkmenistan, Uzbekistan, Kyrgyzstan and Tadjikistan – the Union must face the dilemma of backing less-than-democratic regimes strong enough to push through economic reforms that fairer forms of government might not be able to sustain. The medium-term aim for all the former Soviet republics must be for the Union to negotiate separately tailored agreements for each, while watching and advising as they slowly decide how to cohabit voluntarily amongst themselves. The kind of assistance and cooperation we can offer will vary enormously and it would be a great mistake to seek to impose a common blueprint.

CONCLUSION

The Union's relations with the countries of the former Soviet Union are evolving in a fast-changing scene. In the face of a splintering empire whose subjects have spun centrifugally outwards in blind reaction, only to discover how ill-equipped they are to survive alone in the cold, and despite the revival of old enmities between them, Russia, Ukraine and Belarus have launched a welcome if ambitious blueprint for economic union. But Russo–Ukrainian rivalry, for example over nuclear issues, will not dissolve overnight in spite of their January 1994 agreement. Some of the more far-flung republics, especially those with large Muslim communities, are drawn towards other regional poles of attraction such as Turkey and Iran, even though they as yet make little economic sense.

Clearly, the former USSR is a diverse constellation of countries hitherto yoked together by force. It is unlikely that they would wish to choose, or be wise to choose, the European Union as a model to follow. Unlike post-Communist Eastern Europe, Russia and its neighbours do not share a common continent with a common history. And yet perversely, they did share a common currency, a common army and a common language, albeit grudgingly. Their need to build voluntary ties out of their earlier enforced union, and in spite of their determination to assert their historical independence, is a circle that desperately needs squaring. A question mark will continue to hang over their ties with Europe until they have squared that circle to their own satisfaction. In the meantime, Europe must itself build a vision around that uncertainty, enticing them into the international trading environment by opening its markets, lowering its barriers, and helping Russia to rebuild its industry. For if, while Russia agonizes over its own political future, it grows richer by buying and selling more successfully with the outside world, the future it chooses can reasonably be expected to be less isolationist than its past.

CHAPTER 9

Further Institutional Change

For all its perceived failings, the European Union has proved pretty attractive to its neighbours. Attractive not because they approve of everything it does, but because they recognize the growing influence it exerts over their economic and political lives. In Western Europe, most of them are aligning their own economic rules to those of the Union in order to clear the ground for a pan-European, barrier-free market, the so-called 'European Economic Area'. Austria, Norway, Finland and Sweden have gone one step further, applying to join the EU largely in order to be on the inside when future rules are made; and in Eastern Europe, the new democracies emerging from Communism have made it abundantly clear that they see their future within the Union. This will greatly enrich the geographical, political, cultural and economic fabric of the EC, and must be welcomed. After all, the seeds of the European Union were planted to reunify the entire continent, not through coercion but through the voluntary integration of countries wishing to share their common interests while retaining their historical independence. Furthermore, the Maastricht Treaty decrees that 'Any European State may apply to become a Member of the Union' (Article O of the Treaty), binding the Union to consider calls for membership from anywhere in Europe.

There is a paradox here which, unless handled with the utmost sensitivity, risks turning the Union into a victim of its own success: by proving that it can decide matters collectively and quickly, enhancing the voice of its individual members without drowning them out, the EU has magnetized neighbouring states, making them keen to join. But the very enlargement of the Union could pose the greatest threat of all to its ability to function swiftly and effectively. The Union is already hard enough to manage as it is, making elaborate contortions to accommodate the widely differing views of its twelve member nations. It will prove harder still as three or four more applicants join, although the addition of Austria, Finland, Sweden and Norway will not lead to insuperable problems. If we go beyond that without revising the way we take collective decisions, the wheels of the Union will grind to a halt.

Even if further enlargement would overload the existing decision-making machinery, that is no reason to close the turnstiles after these four have joined. I believe it would be blinkered and historically short-sighted to turn away those countries newly freed from the Soviet yoke on the grounds that the existing space is full to capacity. Membership would stamp the final seal on their return to the family of European nations, just as it did for Spain, Portugal and Greece when they emerged from dictatorship to join the EC. Europe's Union must place political imperatives ahead of institutional problems if it is to be worthy of the name; but those problems do have to be resolved.

At their summit meeting in Copenhagen in June 1993, the EU's heads of state declared that they favour membership for the countries of Central and Eastern Europe when they have built democracies and market economies robust enough to take on board the full panoply of EU rules. The Union must reinforce this by making room now for the day they join, rather than balking at the mere prospect of their membership because they cannot be fitted into the Union's existing architecture. Indeed, the Union's leaders have already agreed to meet in 1996 for their next major Inter-governmental Conference to consider adapting the EU's decision-making machinery for enlargement, as well as tackling other pressing questions about the EU's future. Europe must start preparing the ground for those inter-governmental talks immediately.

In the long run-up to those crucial discussions, countless hobbyhorses will be wheeled out and presented as of the most urgent importance for the future of Europe. The negotiations for the Maastricht Treaty suffered an even greater lack of focus: the economic target at Maastricht – shaping the road towards a monetary and currency union – was always clear, but the exact political goal of the Maastricht talks was altogether hazier. This is largely because the idea of tackling joint foreign and security policy, strengthening democracy and boosting cooperation on home affairs through 'political union', took a while to take shape after Germany had sought their inclusion to counterbalance the predominantly economic and monetary nature of the Maastricht Treaty. We must learn from this experience and focus immediately on the changes needed to accompany enlargement as the central point around which all other questions will turn at the 1996 conference. The institutional implications of a broader Union mark perhaps the biggest hurdle now facing the continent, and all other issues will effectively flow from it.

Some opponents of enlargement often evoke the plight of Europe's smaller countries as a reason for the Union to retain its present size. For the Union to remain effective, they argue, the frail but crucial voices of smaller nations would necessarily be drowned out by their mightier, more vociferous neighours; or if the Union stooped low enough to hear them, it would stumble altogether, never deciding anything. Both of these views are misguided. Luxembourg, with a population of just 350,000, stands alongside Germany, with 80 million inhabitants, defending its banking, farming, cultural and other national interests, and yet this hardly brings the Union to a standstill. EU decision-making may seem byzantine in its complications to the outsider, but this has little to do with the size of its members.

Blockages occur essentially because the basic cogs in the EU's decision-making machine have remained unchanged since 1959. The six founding countries sent nine commissioners to Brussels, now there are seventeen; the number of official EU languages has crept up from four to nine, while the number of countries themselves has doubled. The European Parliament has increased its powers, while lobbies have blossomed to promote interest groups affected by EU laws. And yet amidst all these changes, the EU still runs on the old lines laid down by the Treaty of Rome itself: the rules ensure that the voice of the bigger countries is somewhat lower and that of their smaller neighbours somewhat louder so as to guarantee that all voices are heard, and at a level tolerable to all partners.

Even that basic principle has been challenged, though, in a way that illustrates well just how difficult it will be to adapt the Union to the needs of further enlargement. The debate on institutional change has already started with a suggestion that we should move away from the old form of 'weighted' majority voting, and go over to a system under which today's majority decisions would be taken by a so-called 'double majority' – at least half the Union countries together with at least half its overall population. Nor could those Council decisions currently requiring unanimity be blocked by a veto any more. These would all be taken by a 'super-majority', representing 80 per cent of the population.

This is all part of the discussion about the relative weight of the bigger and smaller countries. Moving over to these 'double' and 'super-qualified' majorities would in effect diminish the weight of the smaller nations. Some people argue that their rights are taken care of because a majority of countries is always required, but if you compare that with the present system, under which Spain, Portugal, the Netherlands and Belgium could block a decision, it is clear that their weight would be reduced if these proposals were implemented.

Obviously, there is a clear attraction to taking decisions by a simple majority of governments and of the populations they represent. It appears to be completely democratic, and is transparent in the way it works, but for the present, I believe that it would be seen by the smaller countries as mortgaging their future to the goodwill of their bigger neighbours, and would be the source of deep resentment within the Union.

But do we really need change now? The original founders of the Union would be the first to argue that the time has come to take change seriously. By and large, the system has functioned well for forty years, but the shape and size of the EU could change so radically that it will soon begin to creak under the strain of enlargement. We need to envisage how the Union will look in ten to twenty years' time, when the newly unified Europe has taken on a more clearly defined shape.

It would be misguided to think of institutional reform as a detached geometrical exercise to avert ill-defined management problems that could only arise some years into the future. The current decision-making system is already overcharged, and needs short-term fine-tuning as well as a longer-term overhaul. There are already severe delays in passing legislation, even legislation that is widely welcomed. Ministers were due to endorse plans for a European Health and Safety Agency in February 1993, for example, but by December that year it had not even passed through the European Parliament, let alone reached the desk of the ministers for final approval.

It is plain that there is a growing gulf separating the institutions taking the decisions and the people whose lives they affect. The EU is unlike any other administration in Europe, and can be hard for ordinary people to fathom. Its

FURTHER INSTITUTIONAL CHANGE

institutions still generate suspicion and distrust, gnawing into the Union's credibility, and must be reformed.

How should we oil the existing Union machine?

To begin with, the Union's institutions need a thorough overhaul to improve their efficiency. When national ministers meet within the decision-making Council of Ministers, for example, their patience is stretched to the limit as they sit for hours through each other's pre-written speeches, few of them adapting their words to the flow of the debate. It is bad enough with twelve countries, but if the Union grows to twenty or twenty-five, ministerial meetings will last for weeks, not hours. Such meetings test the ministers' stamina as much as their patience. When agriculture ministers set annual farm prices, they rarely meet for less than three days on the trot. And when foreign ministers carved up 141 billion ecus worth of aid to regenerate poorer or declining regions for the years 1994 to 1999, they only reached agreement at seven o'clock in the morning after twenty hours of horse-trading. Europe should decide its funding and farm prices on the basis of balanced negotiation, not on stubbornness and stamina.

To start with, preliminary statements could be exchanged in writing, rather than read out aloud. I would also propose the use of 'guillotine' measures. If a debate dragged on beyond a pre-determined period of time, the President of the Council of Ministers could call a vote or force a decision one way or another. Like timed chess moves, this would focus the minds of the ministers, holding them to a deadline but at least allowing them to meet it in a fresh state of mind. The aim is not to improve working conditions for ministers – as an ex-minister, I know better than to think they would receive or deserve much public sympathy – it is about the serious task of tightening up the quality and efficiency of decision-making.

Making the Union more democratic

The stock complaint about the European Union is that its bureaucracy is in surplus and its democracy in deficit. Chapter 2 explored the root causes of the former complaint, particularly the way the public reacts with fear and distrust to a Union it does not understand. As to the more serious allegation that Europe's citizens are deprived, at European level, of the right to control the men and women whose decisions shape their lives, is this allegation justified?

Europe's democracy flows from two sources. To begin with, the Union has its own European Parliament, whose members are directly and democratically elected in each country; and then the Council of Ministers, where most of the power resides, is composed of ministers who are members of democratically elected national governments. Although their procedures may be opaque and their actions far removed from the daily concerns of those who voted them in, neither body can be accused of lacking in democracy. Moreover, the European Parliament was recently bestowed with more powers under the Maastricht Treaty. It has substantially increased authority over the laws that shape the Union's Single Market, where it now enacts these laws in 'co-decision' with the ministers. And it has a growing control over the EU's treaties with the outside world, a power it has used, for example, to block finance to Syria in protest at Syria's record on human rights.

If we cannot improve the democratic structure of these institutions, can we improve their democratic behaviour? For its part, the European Parliament sifts so assiduously through proposed EU rules that it significantly slows matters down; Euro-MPs can hardly be accused of neglecting their electorate. And the Council of Ministers? If the EU tried forcing Westminster, the Assemblée Nationale or the Bundestag to scrutinize EU rules more rigorously, it would be taken as heavy-handed interference from Brussels. Where does that leave Europe's democratic deficit?

The common target of anti-bureaucratic, pro-democratic fervour is the European Commission. Known inaccurately as 'Brussels' or 'The EC', and supposedly teeming with faceless, paper-pushing, power-hungry 'Eurocrats', the Commission must be the world's most experienced scapegoat, the punch-bag against which Europe vents its anger at the ham-fistedness of its own decision-making abilities. The obvious answer, then, should be to turn the Commission into a democratically elected body, but this would alter the current balance funda-mentally, for its founders conceived the EC as a Community of independent states with a central body, the Commission, to power the process of integration along, not to replace them as an embryonic Government of Europe. Elected governments would then accept or reject the Commission's ideas, listening to the views of the European Parliament to give an added democratic voice to the process. The Commission was con-ceived as more than a secretariat, but definitely less than a government. If the Commission was to be the motor, then governments themselves would operate both the throttle and the brake. But if commissioners stood for election, they would be competing for the ear of the electorate with govern-ment ministers and European MPs. If they won enough votes they would gain equal democratic legitimacy, and a Govern-ment of Europe would be born. Many people aspire to such a goal, as the debate over Maastricht shows, but there is nothing even approaching a consensus in favour. Any attempt to force the issue risks turning innocent intentions into devastating results. It would be ironic for the complaints of the Euro-sceptics to lead to a massive new step forward on the road to European integration.

Many doubters of democracy in Europe feel, however,

that their governments do not involve their parliaments enough in the formulation of EU laws. Here, Europe could genuinely deepen its democratic principles both in perception and in reality, and without upsetting the fragile balance on which the Union's integration depends. Europe, therefore, should consider creating a new body representing national parliaments. At the risk of drawing scorn for creating yet another European institution, this should reassure citizens across the continent that working to achieve shared European goals would not jeopardize national diversity nor erode democracy itself in the process.

Putting Europe's parliaments to better use

In every country, many people fear that the Union is driven not by the will of its citizens but by an unguided thirst for more integration. The Union needs to respond to these fears. In 1991, I first proposed the concept of a new body drawing together national parliaments and giving them limited powers over the decision-making process. I believe this should be fleshed out into a full 'Committee of Parliaments' consisting of representatives from each national parliament. National MPs are not elected on their European credentials, but almost all have to scrutinize EU laws nationally at some time or other. If voters felt their local MPs were lending a hand to the process of Euro-legislation, it would greatly strengthen the EU's democracy and enhance its credibility. It would strengthen the tenuous link between the twin strands of elected parliaments – national and European – which often see themselves as in opposition to each other, even though they are doing the same job of ensuring democracy in Europe.

If such a committee were to be more than a talking shop it would need real powers. At Maastricht, government leaders made a half-hearted attempt to plug the gap by attaching a declaration to the new Treaty calling on national and European parliaments to hold a 'Conference of the Parliaments' whenever they saw fit. This is patently not sufficient. Until national parliaments are bound into the grind of the EU's decision mill, their elected representatives will lift their eyes from the crucial texts before them, and merely talk. Their collective wisdom will only lead to concrete improvements to EU rules if they know their views really count.

The Committee of Parliaments should have four rights and duties: the enforcement of the principle of subsidiarity; the right to challenge the legal basis on which laws are drafted; the scrutiny of all laws which carry the Union into new territory; and the scrutiny of laws where, under Maastricht, governments cede the right to act solely between themselves and submit sensitive subjects like asylum and immigration policy to the EU's full decision-making machinery. With these four powers, all of Europe's elected bodies would then be influencing decisions over who does what, and on what grounds; and they would be exerting that influence collectively, as the most democratic tier of authority in the EU.

First, the Committee's role on subsidiarity should be pivotal. The Committee should have the right to call upon the EU's highest legal authority – the European Court of Justice – to adjudicate on the 'subsidiarity test' at any stage in the legislative pipeline. Is it really necessary for action on this question to be taken at European level, they would ask. National governments often fear a loss of sovereignty by stealth: the European Commission and Parliament are suspected of creeping up behind them, manipulating EU rules to push through joint EU decisions which should have remained in national hands. The Committee could allay these anxieties by exercising the right to seek the Court's opinion on a draft law at any stage, preventing ministers from endorsing the measure for up to three months. This would not slow the process down, for proposals could continue through the earlier hoops and hurdles unchecked, but the final decision would remain on hold while the EU's most senior judges determined whether governments should be deciding such matters collectively, or whether it should be left to each government to decide it on a purely national basis. This could in fact accelerate matters, for without such prior screening, the Court could intervene afterwards anyway if requested to do so, leading to a far messier, more time-consuming process of law-making. Nor would it mark a major departure from existing practice. Governments, the Commission or the Council of Ministers can already ask the Court whether international agreements are compatible with Union law.* I am merely seeking a simple, limited extension of this procedure.

The second job of the Committee of Parliaments would be to help ensure that all new EU measures were built on solid legal foundations. Here again it could reassure suspicious governments, for the legal basis so often becomes a battleground for national authorities to fight the European Commission or each other over whether it is a matter for Europe at all, and if so, whether any of them have a right to veto it. Nowhere has this battle raged more virulently than over social policy, where some claim that salaries, working hours and other terms of employment form an inseparable part of their 'health and safety standards', and should therefore be agreed by majority vote (similar health and safety levels throughout the EU are deemed indispensable to the smooth running of the European Single Market). Others argue that

* Article 228, paragraph 6, of the Maastricht Treaty reads: 'The Council, the Commission or a Member State may obtain the opinion of the Court of Justice as to whether an agreement envisaged is compatible with the provisions of this Treaty . . .'

an employee's maternity pay has nothing to do with her health and safety, but rather with her 'rights and interests', over which any country has a veto. The Committee of Parliaments could take a view in such cases, and as with subsidiarity, the Committee could ask the European Court of Justice to give its view on the legal foundation of draft EU laws within three months.

Thirdly, national and European MPs could help steer all laws which took the Union into uncharted European waters. They would give their own view in such delicate situations and that would be a valuable safeguard. When national governments signed the Treaty of Rome, they could only envisage what was inside it, not what would eventually grow out of it. This essentially boils down to the Committee exercising control over the use of Article 235,* which allows governments to step beyond the Treaty in pursuit of their common objectives, so long as they do so unanimously.

Finally, the Committee would have a key role in an altogether more significant area of Union development: when the power exists under Maastricht to shift action from the 'inter-governmental' arena, where governments act between themselves, to the full Union decision-making process, implying a major pooling of national sovereignty. Such areas include asylum, immigration, drug addiction, fraud, rules governing the crossing of external frontiers, and cooperation over law and order. National parliaments have of course approved the Maastricht Treaty as a whole; but as the use of this provision will always involve a major shift of emphasis

---

* Article 235 says. 'If action by the Community should prove necessary to attain, in the course of the operation of the Common Market, one of the objectives of the Community and this Treaty has not provided the necessary powers, the Council shall, acting unanimously on a proposal from the Commission and after consulting the European Parliament, take the appropriate measures.'

away from inter-governmental cooperation and into the realm of joint action launched, drafted and executed through the EU's central decision-making mechanism, it is only right that the representatives of the national parliaments should give their views each and every time.

How would we structure the Committee? If it were too small, it would not gain the experience and authority to carry real weight; but if it were too big, it would risk overriding rather than representing the national parliaments from which it stems. Likewise, if it met too often its members would lose touch with their home parliaments and with the ordinary people they represent, becoming just another Union institution instead. The size and method of operating of the Committee should be determined bearing these factors very much in mind.

The Council of Ministers
(*stopping the big fish from eating the small fry*)

If any reform of the EU's decision-making machine is to be effective, it will have to tackle the most important, but politically controversial, question of all: the way ministers vote. Because the Council of Ministers takes almost all the decisions that affect the lives of Europe's citizens, it needs to operate with maximum efficiency and clarity. And yet at times it is as prone to awkward compromises and outright fudges as it is to swift and decisive action. Why does this happen?

At present, when European ministers gather in Brussels or Luxembourg to decide common rules, they operate within an extremely delicate voting structure deliberately geared in favour of smaller countries. Each country is 'weighted' broadly, though not strictly, according to the strength of its economy and the number of inhabitants (the table opposite illustrates how a country's representation per head of population increases the smaller it is). Ever since the Community was founded, when deciding issues by majority, ministers have needed to muster around 70 per cent of these 'weighted' votes, whatever the number and size of countries in the EU at the time. This so-called 'qualified majority' is not an unacceptably high figure to reach, particularly as the Union always seeks, through consensus, to avoid isolating any of its members anyway. And when treating matters close to the heart of national sovereignty, such as levying taxes, decisions can only be taken unanimously. The rules thus strike a balance between absolute consensus and majority decision-making.

	No. of votes	No. of citizens per vote
Germany, France, Italy, UK	10	6–8 million
Spain	8	5 million
Belgium, Greece, The Netherlands, Portugal	5	2–3 million
Denmark, Ireland	3	1·5 million
Luxembourg	2	200,000

Fifty-four out of the 76 votes are required for a 'qualified majority'. Two bigger countries plus one smaller one can, therefore, oppose measures by forming a 'blocking minority'.

Like instruments in a symphony orchestra, the weighting increases the smaller the countries become: you do not need many trumpets because even a single one will always be heard no matter how large the orchestra and how high the volume; but you do need several desks of violins if they are to avoid being drowned out during the louder movements. The EU's voting structure stops quieter players losing their identity to the bigger brass, avoiding any attempt to constrain smaller countries into a policy they dislike.

Likewise, the voting system aims to stop the small countries outmanoeuvring their larger neighbours by clubbing together. No two small nations can block a proposal; but two larger countries can, with the backing of one small one, thereby preventing a group of smaller countries from rallying support for a measure that their larger partners do not like. The overarching rule within this game of numbers is that no qualified majority is possible without more member states being in favour than against. It is a surprisingly delicate but effective balance which holds the ministers to two basic principles: stopping the big fish from eating the small fry, and preventing the small fry from ganging up on the big fish.

The system is already drawing fire for being too slow. How much slower it will be, and how much less popular it could become, if the Union fails to reform it before admitting new countries. On the other hand, as I have already pointed out, schemes designed simply to enhance the power of the larger countries are bound to arouse enormous suspicion.

Instead we need to develop more sophisticated machinery, adding another cog to accelerate decision-making *without* upsetting the balance between decision-makers as their numbers increase. Instead of dividing the growing number of tasks into two categories, namely those that strike to the core of national sovereignty and the rest, we need to build a new three-tier voting system.

Tier one could cover a strict definition of measures which would facilitate the purchase and sale of goods and services anywhere in the EU, and help capital to flow freely between countries; these would include internal market measures themselves, health and safety at work, and farm and fisheries policy. It would also include the fixing of normal trade tariffs governing the access of imports into the Union. These measures would be subject to 'low majority' voting, making it harder than at present for governments to muster a blocking minority in such cases.

Tier two could govern matters which touched the life of the individual citizen, such as social rules and environmental control. It could also include exceptional trade measures, such as those the Union sometimes needs in order to limit trade, for example when European industry suffers under a sudden surge of very low-cost imports. Tier two issues would still be subject to a 'high majority' vote, with the bar set higher than in tier one, making that majority harder to achieve, though still impossible for a single country to block.

Tier three should cover the levying of taxes, all moves towards Economic and Monetary Union, boosting the size of the Union's budget, and all laws on visas and immigration. Governments would retain their right of veto over these and other issues where core sovereignty is at stake.

There is ample room for prolonged discussions about the actual number of votes that should be required for the two types of majorities, but the principle seems to me a sound one. Moreover, the new powers I suggest for the Committee of Parliaments would help reassure governments wary of the misuse of the inevitably more complex system by which legislation was put into a particular category. This system would expose more policies to a majority vote, accelerating decision-making as a result, while reflecting the national sensitivity of issues more closely.

Expanding the rotating presidency

Every six months, a new country climbs into the presidential cockpit of the European Union, taking over from its alphabetical predecessor (in its own language, that is. The Euro-alphabet can cause some surprises: Greece and Spain may seem at opposite ends of the alphabet, but '*Ellas*' and '*España*' are adjacent, so one follows the other.) The rotating presidency is far more than pure ceremony, as it chairs meetings, fixes agendas and crafts compromises between EU states as well as with the European Commission in order to chivvy countries forward, thereby securing agreements and making a success of its six months in the chair. In the past, each nation would operate in near-isolation from the rest, seeking to impose its stamp on the Union but failing to do so, largely because it lacked time to make a real mark on its own. Continuity was then conceived through the creation of the 'Troika', whereby the president is helped with planning and accompanied on diplomatic missions by representatives from the countries immediately before and after in the alphabetical queue.

This will need adapting as the Union expands in number. Some suggest extending the term to a full year, but this would remove one key purpose of the rotation: to give countries reasonably frequent opportunities to advance the Union in their own particular way. At present there is usually one large country in the Troika at any one time, but even that will change. With Luxembourg, the Netherlands, Norway, Portugal and Sweden all side-by-side in alphabetical order, three small countries would be at the helm for eighteen months. And it is not totally unfeasible to imagine Latvia, Lithuania and Luxembourg representing a greatly increased EU on the world stage. The only solution must be to transform the Troika into a 'Quad' and ensure that one major player always stands alongside the other three. A bigger country would join the presidency, in rotation, every time the alphabet produced three smaller states in a row. Bigger nations would contribute their broader diplomatic network, greater resources and added weight in international fora to the representation of the Union. This would strengthen the presidency without upsetting the crucial balance between nations large and small on which the Union's general acceptability depends.

The European Parliament

Before Maastricht, the European Parliament's real power lay predominantly in its right to reject the EU's annual budget, demand a second reading on Single Market measures and reject them if it felt strongly enough, or sack the Commission *en bloc*. It did the first rarely, and the second ever more frequently, but it never did the third. Maastricht has given it far greater powers, which I strongly welcome, as experience shows that any parliament acts more responsibly the more power it has. The European Parliament emerged from Maastricht* with what amounts to a share in deciding rules governing the Single Market, the service industries, the free movement of workers, the right of companies and people to set up anywhere in the Union, the EU's research and environment programmes, and its educational and cultural policies. This power amounts to an effective veto. Every use of this veto requires the vote of half of all MEPs, no matter how many are present at the time, making it seem quite a feat; and yet parliamentary motions regularly muster at least that majority already.

The Parliament now exercises a stronger grip over the Commission too. It has won the right to approve the commissioners nominated by governments before they take office. Whoever doubts the potential force of such a change should cast his eye across the Atlantic to see just how deftly the American Senate wields its power to confirm presidential

* Under the so-called 'co-decision' procedure, the Parliament's first reading is only advisory. But when the Council has reached a 'common position' (agreement after the Parliament's first reading), the Parliament's powers grow. After the second reading, the Council and Parliament will sit down together to discuss their differences over a draft. If they succeed in resolving them, they adopt the act jointly. If they fail, however, either side can reject the text, and the legislation falls. This effectively gives the European Parliament the power of veto.

appointees. The European Parliament can only accept or reject commissioners *en bloc*, so it will most probably exert its influence by scrutinizing the policies promised by an incoming Commission as the basis for giving its assent.

But if Europe has given its common Parliament more power, why has it not rendered it more accountable for its actions? At present there is no guarantee that the policies it supports will form a consistent whole. For example, together with the Council, the Parliament helps fix the size of the Union budget and the way it is spent, but it is not responsible to the European electorate for the taxes needed to finance it. These are shortcomings in the system, not faults in the MEPs or political parties operating within it. None the less, as parliamentary power over the Commission and government ministers becomes more apparent, there will be growing calls for a mechanism to ensure that Europe follows a consistent and continuous policy. In most Union countries, parliament can ultimately be dissolved and fresh elections called, usually by the head of state, in order to end gridlock between the legislature and the executive. Finding a way of agreeing to the dissolution of the European Parliament would be formidably difficult: who would initiate such a move, who would decide it and by what majority? I do not propose any such mechanism here, nor am I seeking to scare Europe's directly chosen representatives off their new-found powers before they have even begun. But as a democratic body grows stronger, it is more likely to come into conflict with the executive, and it may be necessary in the future to find a way to consult the electorate if gridlock between the institutions does occur.

Avoiding too many committees

Euro-cynics often remark that, if in doubt, the European Union forms another committee. Maastricht did just that, though not out of doubt but through a desire to reflect the growing identity of Europe's regions within their country and within Europe as a whole. EU leaders created the Committee of the Regions to reflect this new voice at European level. But Europe's regions differ widely in role and status across the Union, largely stemming from history: Germany was for long a federation of semi-independent states, while France has been a highly centralized country since the reign of Louis XIV. German regions today run schools and universities, transport, broadcasting, and planning permission, for example, while in France, despite the trend towards decentralization, central powers channelled through the central government's representatives remain substantial. Naturally, governments' eagerness for the Committee of the Regions matched the level of regional autonomy over which they preside: Germany made its support for Maastricht conditional on the creation of such a Committee. There is undoubtedly a case for it, although the sheer diversity between the regions could make it difficult for them to speak with a common voice.

Just as Europe plants new committees to suit the changing climate, so it should prune the old ones and if necessary uproot them. In an effort to bring voices other than governments and the European Parliament into the decision-making process, the Union created the Economic and Social Committee. In language redolent of the corporatist philosophy of the 1960s, it names three constituent groups – employers, workers and 'various interests'.* Its 'counsellors' nominated by these

---

* Employers' representatives come from private and public industry, chambers of commerce, small business, the wholesale and retail trade, transport, banking, agriculture and tourism. Workers are picked from major trade union confederations, or from sectoral union groupings. 'Various interests' include farmers, craftworkers, traders, lawyers, consumers, scientists, teachers, cooperatives and the non-profit-making sector, family organizations and environmental lobbies.

groups draft extremely well-researched opinions on almost all EU measures before they become law.

But Europe's real decision-makers, the national ministers themselves, pay it lip-service and little more, even on matters where it has considerable know-how, such as the European Single Market. The Treaty of Rome provides for ECOSOC, as it is known, to speak for 'the various categories of economic and social activity . . . and representatives of the general public'. But those voices are now heard through other channels, notably the European Parliament itself. Obviously employers, unions, consumers and others need consulting on laws that affect their lives, but they now speak very effectively through their own powerful lobbies. Do we still need a formal EU committee to do the same job? There can be few bodies in Europe where so much expertise and hard graft goes to so little effect. We have to ask ourselves whether, if we were building the Union from scratch, we would invent the Economic and Social Committee today. I fear that my own answer would be no.

Should the Commission be less powerful or more efficient?

There are two common criticisms of the European Commission, both exaggerated, one contradicting the other, and which reveal a telling public ambivalence towards the Union itself. To some it is lazy, bureaucratic and spendthrift, and by implication ineffectual. To others it is scheming, ambitious and self-inflating, implying that it is hyper-efficient. To the former, it is a drain on the public purse but not a danger to democracy and sovereignty; it needs a few stern lessons in housekeeping and nothing more. But this would worry the latter camp, who believe that streamlining a wickedly efficient Commission would make matters worse. It needs watching closely, for Brussels, they believe, is the Artful Dodger of EU decision-making, pick-pocketing governments of their rightful powers because it knows the backstreets of European law better than they do. Who is right?

History may help explain this ambivalence. Up to 1987, the Commission was often little more than a secretariat, watching resignedly as governments relegated its proposals to the back burner. Since the Single European Act in 1986, the Commission has made a come-back under the presidency of Jacques Delors. It has managed to reclaim its status as a political body, responsible for motoring the member states towards further integration just as the founding countries of the Community had intended in the Treaty of Rome; but governments still operate the brakes, as they always have.

The Commission is only restoring its original role, not increasing it, but this is interpreted as a new upsurge in power which needs curtailing. The Commission's zeal has certainly sometimes been excessive, but it has not, in fact, amassed vast new powers and does not need to have its wings clipped. Indeed, governments have already ring-fenced many of the Commission's fabled powers. When the Union manages its agricultural markets or agrees spending on foreign aid programmes, for example, government officials can approve measures even before the Commission decides, and if the Commission tries to oppose them, the case goes automatically to the ministers to decide.

The Commission needs rather to retain its existing powers, notably the sole right to initiate proposals, while greatly streamlining its ability to act efficiently and responsibly within those powers but not beyond them. This is doubly important if it is to play its role in helping to keep the Union on a steady course as it grows in size. It will also help improve the Commission's battered image in the countries it serves. By all means governments should criticize the Commission when it oversteps its rightful role, but the more they lambast it for implementing the powers bestowed upon it by their predecessors, the weaker its ability to protect the delicate balance of interests between countries on which all governments depend. Europe needs a high-quality, independent and motivated executive at the centre of the pitch, not to centralize Europe by replacing the players, but to keep the playing field level between them.

The task of improving the Commission must begin with governments themselves. In fact, it has already begun, as Maastricht will streamline the process of appointing the commissioners: governments must now consult the Parliament on their choice of Commission President, and once he has been chosen they must then consult him on the candidates they pick to become his team of commissioners. Finally, the team as a whole needs the Parliament's formal go-ahead before taking up office.

Governments must continue to realize that it is in their own self-interest to appoint commissioners with all the right aptitudes for the work they will face. To give one simple but important example: a commissioner with poor linguistic skills is substantially less capable of influencing Commission policy. There are notable exceptions, and the Union's formidably sophisticated interpretation service makes it possible for commissioners to operate solely in their own tongue. But monolingual commissioners are handicapped in the crucial informal contacts that back up the EU's formal policy-making. Equally, previous ministerial experience is increasingly accepted as essential, equipping commissioners with a political understanding and sensitivity commensurate with the Commission's role as a political body.

Enlargement will bring the need to adapt the number of commissioners and the division of their responsibilities. At present, each country has at least one commissioner and the largest five countries – Germany, France, Britain, Italy and

Spain – each have two. If this system continues as the Union expands, the Commission will grow too big and unwieldy to perform effectively. The idea of the bigger members forfeiting their right to a second commissioner to slim down numbers has already been floated widely, but this will not solve the problem as new countries join.

The greater the Union's responsibilities and the broader its tasks become, the stronger the case for greater hierarchy within the Commission itself, along the lines of a national government. Currently there is a horizontal structure beneath the President, giving equal weight to commissioners irrespective of their portfolio. This can produce fair, balanced and 'collegiate' debates, which is crucial, but it does not generate fast and effective decisions. And in foreign affairs, it can prevent the Commission from representing the Union in several places across the globe at the same time while maintaining its cohesiveness back in Brussels. Europe's partners will negotiate more readily with commissioners than with officials, not because the latter are less competent but because a minister is expected to engage with his hierarchical equal during serious negotiations.

If the Commission were to reduce the number of its departments, it could concentrate its political energies on the most pressing issues while sharpening the focus of its legislative and managerial responsibilities. This could help to avoid the proliferation of unnecessary EU laws. At the same time, by splitting its ranks into full and junior commissioners, it could ensure much more effective political control over the actions of its departments. In all modern democracies, senior ministers have junior counterparts beneath them, but both still participate in deciding the direction policy should take.

Let us suppose there was one commissioner per country, with ten full commissioners and the rest fulfilling the junior role. This model could work as effectively today as when the Union grows in size. All countries would be represented in the Commission, but not always with a senior commissioner. Bigger countries would always have a full commissioner, while the smaller ones would rotate between senior and junior commissioners, roughly along the lines of permanent and rotating members of the UN Security Council. Full commissioners would hold the most important portfolios and would be reinforced by junior colleagues.

The precise distribution of portfolios and the balance between senior and junior commissioners should be flexible depending on the changing needs of the Union. The following illustration shows how the Commission's main present-day responsibilities could be adequately carved out into ten key areas, with one full commissioner for each:

> President, handling coordination of the entire Commission
> External relations, including development
> Economic affairs, including EMU
> Environment
> Transport and regional policy
> Agriculture and fisheries
> Industry, the internal market and energy
> Competitiveness, including social policy, education and research
> Competition policy
> Budget, financial control, personnel and administration.

Each full commissioner would have two votes, and each junior one just a single vote. Commission proposals would have to muster at least half the number of heads as well as half the votes before being approved. A junior commissioner should not be allowed to vote against a full member who heads his department, because this could obviously cause considerable embarrassment.

Reforming the Commission in this way could kill several birds with one stone: it could streamline its administration, accelerate the reallocation of staff and funds between competing priorities, and reassure EU governments that more commissioners would lead to an improvement, rather than an increase, in laws and actions; it would also enable the Commission to present a more coherent image to the outside world.

Conclusion

The weighing scales of European politics are so finely poised that even the slightest jog to the institutions binding Europe together can tip them off-balance in the eyes of suspicious governments. The Community has tackled institutional reform before, when it signed the Single European Act and then the Maastricht Treaty, but on both occasions fear of upsetting the political balance made the Community shy away from some of the major mechanical changes needed to make it more efficient. While the Community remained of manageable size, Europe could muddle through with its old institutions untouched. Substantial further enlargement makes change essential.

Europe needs to reform the behaviour as well as the structure of its institutions. Bleary-eyed ministers make more mistakes than alert ones, so they should craft their compromises within a time limit, using the guillotine if necessary. It must also get national parliaments much more involved in European affairs, in detail, providing far more democratic scrutiny of EU rules. The creation of a Committee of Parliaments would keep EU powers in check while keeping all MPs in touch. Europe's democracy is more disjointed than in deficit.

Some of the most useful improvements to the system do not concern democracy at all. The EU's public credibility will hinge less upon democratic reform than upon Europe's ability to use the prospect of enlargement in order to increase its sheer efficiency, by making a series of mechanical changes to the way its institutions take decisions. But no matter how big the Union eventually becomes, all its members must retain a seat in all its institutions. The Commission for its part needs to become more operational, with two ranks of commissioner as in national governments, and by fitting the people round the policies rather than vice versa.

Above all, the changes in the voting system in the Council of Ministers are essential if decision-making is not to be paralysed. Europe will only be able to 'deepen' and 'widen' at the same time if the fish swim together whatever their size, and the shoal moves just as fast however big it grows.

CHAPTER 10
Conclusions

In this book I have tried to explain the reasons for the confidence-sapping uncertainties and nervousness aroused by the debates which raged up and down Europe in the context of Maastricht; but also to show why and how that time of polarization can now be left behind us. Not because the difficulties are over or because there will not be a rich store of new controversies to replace the old ones. But rather because despite the formidable new agenda facing Europe, there is every reason to believe we can tackle it with confidence, provided we are prepared to learn the lessons of the past couple of years and use the tools we have at our disposal with a judicious combination of vision and moderation. The successful conclusion of the Uruguay Round is a highly relevant recent illustration of the fact that with self-confidence, clarity of purpose and unity of resolve Europe *can* achieve ambitious objectives and emerge from its recent slough of despair.

How can we apply that lesson more widely? To me it has always been clear that to achieve our objectives we need both to preserve the strengths and vitality of the nation states and to draw on the resources of the common, democratically controlled institutions which, to paraphrase Jean Monnet, our continent requires to promote effectively the common weal. The states which have established the European Union will each retain their own clear identity, personality and wide-ranging spheres of independence. Common sense, however, continues to suggest that there is also much that can usefully –

indeed, most sensibly – be done at the European level. The old structures have their continuing validity, but they need over them, if our interests are to have optimal protection, a firm European roof.

Certainly it is important that decisions which can better be taken at national or local level should not be taken in Brussels. But it is important, too, to remember that the main reason for the creation of the European Union was the conviction of those who created it, and of the others who joined it later, that there was also much that could only be done, or could be better done, by working in common. The precise extent of the area of Union activity will always be the subject of legitimate debate, and the right terrain for Union action will vary over the years, with new fields of activity sometimes moving into the ambit of the Union and other ones moving out of it.

So long as the movement is not all one way, there is no reason why the Union should become or be regarded as a leviathan, forever devouring new fields of competence. Contrary to some of the wilder flights of fancy of the opponents of Maastricht, the European Commission is no incipient tyrant, the European Court of Justice no enemy of the European peoples, and the European Parliament, for all its inexperience, not the illegitimate cuckoo in the parliamentary nest some would make it out to be. If the checks and balances built in to the system are properly used, and if those at the helm exercise a degree of self-restraint, the Union institutions can play their proper role as the guarantors of fair play and even dealing: the architects, groundsmen and referees who between them ensure both that the European playing field is made and kept level, and that those who play on it stick to the democratically agreed rules.

Let us by all means, as the Treaty of Maastricht specifies, respect the need for decisions to be taken as closely as possible to the citizen. But where the member states cannot by themselves, as the Treaty puts it, sufficiently achieve the objectives of the proposed action, and that action, by reason of its scale or effects, can be better achieved by the Union, then the Union should not hesitate to play its part.

In doing so it needs to respect four guiding principles: not just subsidiarity, but also democracy, tolerance and fidelity to the fundamental purpose of the Union. The aim must be a policy programme constructed on that basis, which is flexible enough to accommodate, where necessary, a measure of variable geometry but cohesive enough to ensure the achievement of our principal objectives.

The greatest challenge confronting us is to find remedies for Europe's lagging economic performance, for the root causes of our economic malaise. To do that we must perfect the Single Market and strengthen the application of our competition rules, while pressing forward as fast as is prudently possible towards Economic and Monetary Union – all within the wider context of the drive to open up world markets and thus facilitate sustainable long-term growth.

At the same time we need also to remember the importance of stewardship, of ensuring that the human and natural resources of our continent are given, without being over-regulated, the protection they require. That must involve finding the right balance between our priorities, and between intervention and abstention, ushering in the future while taking care to safeguard those parts of our patrimony that we cannot afford to lose.

We will need, too, to do all we can to strengthen and make effective the common foreign and security policy of the European Union, which is currently only in its infancy, with one of our main purposes being the restoration of the full integrity of the Europe sundered in two by the Cold War.

Above all, as we move forward with the implementation

of Maastricht and prepare for the 1996 review of our institutional framework, we must take great care not to push for perfection too hard or too fast. The construction of Europe will continue to benefit enormously from a strong idealism on the part of its architects, but we need also to bear in mind Immanuel Kant's saying that 'Out of the crooked timber of humanity no straight thing was ever made.' We must work with the grain of the people of Europe, and not against it. That is the main lesson to be derived from the reaction against Maastricht over the past two years in so many parts of Europe.

We must not, however, lose our idealism, our determination, our purpose or our vision. In Zurich in 1946, surveying the chaotic state of Europe at the end of the Second World War, Winston Churchill put the case for 'a European group which could give a sense of enlarged patriotism and common citizenship to the distracted peoples of this turbulent and mighty continent'. Nearly half a century later, our peoples are again prey to many uncertainties. It is up to the statesmen of today to respond by charting a way forward which is both navigable and inspiring. There is no shortage of opportunities. Let us seize them with both hands.